Discovering Nature with Young Children

Trainer's Guide

OTHER BOOKS IN THE YOUNG SCIENTIST SERIES:

Exploring Water with Young Children
Exploring Water with Young Children Trainer's Guide
Exploring Water with Young Children Trainer's Set (Video and Guide)

by Ingrid Chalufour and Karen Worth
Education Development Center, Inc.

Building Structures with Young Children
Building Structures with Young Children Trainer's Guide
Building Structures with Young Children Trainer's Set (Video and Guide)

by Ingrid Chalufour and Karen Worth
Education Development Center, Inc.

discovering nature with young children

The *Young* *Scientist* *Series*

Ingrid Chalufour and Karen Worth
Education Development Center, Inc.

Redleaf Press
St. Paul, Minnesota
www.redleafpress.org

Published by Redleaf Press
a division of Resources for Child Caring
10 Yorkton Court
St. Paul, MN 55117
Visit us online at www.redleafpress.org

Written by Ingrid Chalufour and Karen Worth with Robin Moriarty, Jeff Winokur, and Sharon Grollman.

Redleaf Press books are available at a special discount when purchased in bulk for special premiums and sales promotions. For details, contact the sales manager at 800-423-8309.

This book was written with the support of National Science Foundation Grant ESI-9818737. However, any opinions, findings, conclusions, and/or recommendations herein are those of the authors and do not necessarily reflect the views of NSF.

ISBN 1-929610-39-4

contents

acknowledgments

The Young Scientist Series was developed by the project staff of the Tool Kit for Early Childhood Science Education housed at Education Development Center, Inc. (EDC), with funding from the National Science Foundation.

Numerous educators and consultants contributed to the development and field testing of the series. We would like to thank the following people for their contributions to this work.

DEVELOPMENT TEACHERS

Cindy Hoisington
Lucia McAlpin
Carole Moyer
Rebecca Palacios
Susan Steinsick

PILOT TEACHERS

Colette Auguste
Liana Bond
Imelda DeCosta
Marlene Dure
Frank Greene
Karen Hoppe
Terry Küchenmeister
Stuart Lui
Maureen McIntee
Susan Miller
Katherine O'Leary
Carolyn Robinson
Ellen Sulek
Laurie Wormstead
Tiffany Young

FIELD TEST SITES

Bainbridge Island Child Care
   Centers, Bainbridge Island, WA
Barre Town School, Barre, VT
Berlin Elementary School,
   Berlin, VT
Blackwater Community School,
   Coolidge, AZ
Blue Hill Avenue Early Education
   Center, Boston, MA

Bright Horizons at Preston
   Corners, Cary, NC
Childspace Day Care Centers,
   Philadelphia, PA
City of Phoenix Head Start,
   Phoenix, AZ
Cisco Family Connection Bright
   Horizons, Milpitas, CA
East Montpelier Elementary
   School, East Montpelier, VT
Epic Head Start, Yakima, WA
Fort Worth Museum of Science
   and History, Fort Worth, TX
Four Corners School, East
   Montpelier, VT
K–5 Inquiry-Based Science
   Program, Seattle Public
   Schools, WA
Louisiana Tech University Early
   Childhood Education Center,
   Ruston, LA
Motorola Childcare and Education
   Center, Schaumburg, IL
Pasadena Unified School District,
   Pasadena, CA
Phoenix Head Start, Phoenix, AZ
Portage Private Industry Council
   Head Start, Ravenna, OH
School for Early Learning, Spring
   Branch Independent School
   District, Houston, TX
Thomson Early Childhood Center,
   Seattle, WA
UMC Child Development Lab,
   Columbia, MO

Valle Imperial Project in Science,
   El Centro, CA
William H. Rowe School,
   Yarmouth, ME
Young Achievers Science and
   Mathematics Pilot School,
   Boston, MA

ADVISORY BOARD MEMBERS

Douglas Clements
David Dickinson
George Forman
Linda French
Marilou Hyson
Stephanie Johnson
Diane Levin
Mary Jane Moran
Carolyn Vieria
Sandra Williams
Diane Willow

CONSULTANTS

Mary Eisenberg
Pat Fitzsimmons
Ben Mardell
Janet Sebell

We also would like to acknowledge the following people at EDC:

Erica Fields, Research Assistant
Kerry Ouellet, Editor and
   Production Manager
Susan Weinberg, Senior
   Administrative Assistant

introduction

"The Young Scientist professional development materials were very, very helpful. As an instructor I knew just what to do and the teachers really enjoyed the workshops. I feel their excitement has transferred to the children. Both boys and girls are interested in and excited about their science explorations."
—EARLY CARE AND EDUCATION PROGRAM DIRECTOR

Cindy Richards, director of the West Side Early Childhood Center, found that the current trends toward standards and child outcomes caused her to question what children were really learning. Teachers were concentrating on helping children to recognize letters, rather than encouraging children to look at books or use print to communicate their own ideas. Her teachers would set up a science table, but children rarely spent time there or investigated a topic in-depth. Ms. Richards had been sending teachers to workshops for years—hoping her teachers would learn new strategies for improving early literacy, science, and math—but the effects were rarely apparent in the classroom. Ms. Richards felt the time had come to change her approach but she was unsure what she could do to improve teaching and learning in her program.

Then she was asked if her program would field-test the Young Scientist teacher guides—on water, living things, and structures—and the accompanying professional development program. Ms. Richards was reluctant at first, wondering if this was just one more gimmick, just one more shot in the dark. Flipping through the materials, she was surprised to see how extensive the program was—which was a bit daunting. But she hoped its comprehensive nature might lead to the changes she was looking for. So she said yes. She found that the hands-on exploration built teachers' understanding of the science content, inquiry process, and the Young Scientist approach to teaching. The video vignettes helped teachers connect this content approach to their own teaching practice. Ms. Richards notes, "One of the most important things I learned was the importance of time. It takes time to learn new approaches and integrate them into teaching practice. It takes time to provide teachers with the ongoing support they need to sustain successful change." As a result of participating in this professional development program, Ms. Richards sees evidence of teachers applying what they have learned. Teachers are engaging children in in-depth science explorations over time. Teachers' conversations with children don't just focus on management now (such as "Make sure to put the blocks away when you're done"), but on what children are doing and thinking (such as "How could you make the building stronger?"). For the first time, many teachers are documenting children's observations and ideas and using them to extend learning. This has been evident not only in science, but in other domains as well. Ms. Richards reflects, "Teachers see their role, their curriculum, and the children in a new way. For the first time, they are recognizing and capitalizing on the science in the everyday, which helps them to guide children's science learning more effectively. At the same time, they appreciate what children notice and wonder about, what they can do, and understand."

Others who have field-tested the Young Scientist series have had similar reactions:

"I found it really easy to follow. Everything was very clear. Anybody could use it. The teachers didn't lose interest. They really liked the hands-on parts, and they were very engaged in the reflective discussions."
—PUBLIC SCHOOL ADMINISTRATOR

"When I read through the workshops, they looked so good, I decided we needed to do them all!"
—HEAD START DIRECTOR

The Young Scientist

The above vignette suggests the excitement that can be generated when teachers really enjoy learning about and trying out new teaching approaches. In order to build the knowledge and skills teachers need to implement an inquiry-based science curriculum, the Young Scientist provides both teacher guides and a comprehensive set of training materials for each of three science explorations:

- *Discovering Nature with Young Children* invites children to assume the role of a naturalist as they observe and learn about plants and animals in the immediate outdoors, as well as in their own classrooms.
- *Exploring Water with Young Children* helps children examine the properties of water.
- *Building Structures with Young Children* engages children in investigating the relationships between building materials and design and the strength and stability of the structures.

DEVELOPMENT AND TESTING

The Young Scientist is a result of a four-year grant funded by the National Science Foundation. It draws on current understanding of best practice in science teaching and learning. Key to the development process has been the involvement of practitioners and experts from the field who have helped us design our approach, review draft documents, and test the curriculum and professional development materials. The final stage in this process was a national field test conducted from 2001 and 2002, in nineteen early childhood programs including Head Start, pre-K, child care centers, and private nursery schools. Program directors, education managers, and curriculum coordinators from these programs planned and implemented the training activities. Ninety teachers participated in the workshops and used the teacher's guides in their classrooms. Results revealed that some combination of the workshops and more informal support was important to help teachers apply their new learning in the classroom. Moreover, participants reported evidence of science learning in children's questions, observations, and discussions.

Overview of the Trainer's Guide

Teachers often feel insecure and inadequate about their own understanding of science concepts and do not realize how they can learn through inquiry and then use their new understanding in the classroom. These training materials focus on helping teachers begin to gain an understanding of the underlying science concepts in the *Discovering Nature with Young Children* teacher's guide and learn to use that guide to facilitate children's inquiry.

This guide includes all of the instructions, print, and video materials you will need to provide rich professional development experiences for teachers as they implement the *Discovering Nature with Young Children* teacher's guide in their classrooms. When workshops and guided discussions are combined with mentoring over time, your training program will lead to a quality science education program.

The trainer's guide has four components:

- A set of six **BASIC WORKSHOPS:** These workshops use hands-on experiences and reflective conversations to provide teachers with the following: a practical understanding of the science content and inquiry process that will inform their teaching; help in recognizing the science in children's work; and help in guiding children's explorations. These workshops also provide an overview of all sections of the teacher's guide.

- Eight **ADVANCED WORKSHOPS:** These workshops use samples of children's work and conversations to help teachers build a practical understanding of their multifaceted role as facilitators of science inquiry.

- A structure for **GUIDED DISCUSSIONS:** These discussions provide a forum for small groups of teachers to use classroom documentation to stimulate collaborative reflection on their own science teaching and plan new and more effective approaches.

- A description of a **MENTORING PROGRAM:** This section helps mentors use classroom observations and conferencing to support teachers with their individual challenges and help them assess their teaching and refine their practice.

The following sections will help you plan and implement your program:

- **PLANNING AN EFFECTIVE PROFESSIONAL DEVELOPMENT PROGRAM** (below) will help you select the appropriate components and schedule your events.

- **GETTING STARTED** (p. 6) describes a three-step process for preparing yourself for conducting the basic and advanced workshops.

- **RESOURCES** (p. 191) offers a range of tools, including descriptions of each of the instructional strategies used in the workshops, guidance and forms for evaluating teacher growth and planning guided discussions, a log of the video vignettes, and a bibliography of readings for you and for teachers.

Planning an Effective Professional Development Program

These comprehensive training materials, designed to support teacher implementation of the *Discovering Nature with Young Children* teacher guide, can be adapted to the needs of your particular program and teachers. We suggest you plan a three-stage program.

1. Help your teachers become familiar with the teacher's guide and the science concepts and inquiry process at the heart of *Discovering Nature with Young Children*.

2. Help teachers build their capacity as inquiry-based science teachers.

3. Sustain progress you have made and support teachers as they continue to refine their science teaching practice.

Implement these stages one at a time, based on your assessment of teacher's strengths and needs.

Stage 1: Learn to Use the Teacher Guide

Use the six basic workshops to help teachers understand life science concepts, the inquiry process, and the teacher's guide. These workshops, which consist of one three-hour introduction and five one-and-a-half-hour sessions, provide the knowledge and experience teachers need as they begin to implement the teacher's guide. When scheduling the workshops consider several factors:

- Teachers will need the first three workshops before they begin using *Discovering Nature with Young Children*. These workshops will introduce the science concepts and the nature of science inquiry, help them prepare their environment, and provide an overview of open exploration.

- Teachers will need workshops 4 and 5 before moving on to focused exploration. These two workshops will provide a hands-on focused exploration and an overview of the purpose and teacher role in this stage of the exploration, preparing them to facilitate deeper investigations. Try not to wait more than three weeks between workshop 3 and 4. Teachers will need to understand how to deepen children's investigation and apply this in the classroom, otherwise the children will lose interest.

- Find ways to keep this focus on science teaching and learning in the foreground of your program's activity. Check in with teachers regularly to see how things are going in their classrooms. Do they have the materials they need? Are they finding enough time for exploration and science talks? Are the children engaged? Use mentoring or guided discussions to maintain the focus if there are extended periods between the workshops.

- Consider your climate. *Discovering Nature with Young Children* requires outdoor investigation of living things. In climates with cold winters, teachers should begin open exploration no later than early October so that animals and live plants can still be found outdoors. They can either continue with focused exploration indoors when it gets cold or return to the exploration in the spring when plant and animal life are accessible outdoors.

Program Sample Schedules

1. The teachers in the sample program were able to schedule most of their training sessions during naptime when they would otherwise be planning. They were also able to fit in a full-day session before the school year began. The director wanted to provide individual support from the beginning by scheduling two observation and conference sessions with each teacher during stage 1. The first helped teachers make the transition to focused exploration. The second supported their efforts to integrate representation and science talks into their regular routine and to use them effectively for science learning.

SCIENCE EXPLORATIONS WORKSHOP SCHEDULE

September 3
9:00 A.M.–3:00 P.M.
Workshops 1 and 2: Introduction and
Getting Ready

September 12
1:30–3:00 P.M.
Workshop 3: Open Exploration

Observation and conferences will be scheduled with each classroom from September 26
through October 10.

October 3
1:30–3:00 P.M.
Workshop 4: Focused Exploration of Animals

October 10
1:30–3:00 P.M.
Workshop 5: Focused Exploration

Observation and conferences will be scheduled with each teacher from October 10
through November 7.

November 7
1:00–2:30 P.M.
Focused Exploration of Plants

2. In another center there is no time during the day for workshops, but the teachers were eager to implement the program in their classrooms. The director offered pizza dinner and baby-sitting in exchange for their participation after the center closed. The director did her first observation and conference at the end of the series to help her prepare for stage 2.

HIGHLAND CHILD CARE CENTER'S SCIENCE EXPLORATIONS WORKSHOPS

Everybody Attend!!!
Pizza served at 6:30 P.M.
Workshops begin promptly at 7:00 P.M.

September 4*, 11, 18, October 9, 16, and November 13

*Note: The September 4 workshop is 6:00 to 9:00 P.M.

STAGE 2: BUILD CAPACITY AS INQUIRY-BASED SCIENCE TEACHERS

If you have completed the basic workshops, teachers should be beginning to use the guide and this approach to engaging children in the exploration of the plant and animal world. Use "Assessing Teacher Growth" (in "Resources," p. 202) to assess their practice. Work with your teachers to identify appropriate goals. "Science Teacher Development Plan" ("Resources," p. 210) is a useful resource when you are considering next steps and the level of support to provide as you move on. Teachers still at the beginning stage might need some help, individually or in a small group, with the goals that best meet their needs. The chapters on mentoring and guided discussion will help you plan your work with them.

Many teachers will be ready to move onto the advanced workshops after completing the basic ones. As you plan consider the following:

- Start with the first workshop, "Creating a Culture of Inquiry About Nature," which includes an individual needs assessment that will help you better understand how teachers perceive their needs and interests.

- Plan a sequence of workshops that best reflects the needs and interests identified by them and you.

- Allow time in between workshops (at least one month) for teachers to implement the approaches presented.

- Use mentoring or guided discussions to support teachers' efforts in between the workshops.

STAGE 3: PROVIDE ONGOING SUPPORT AS TEACHERS REFINE THEIR PRACTICE

If you have not used guided discussions and mentoring before completing the basic and advanced workshops, now is the time. Regular opportunities to talk about science teaching and learning will be key to sustaining and building on the gains you have made. Guided discussions provide a vehicle for encouraging documentation and analysis of the teaching and learning going on in your program. At the same time, you will be encouraging teacher collaboration and providing a vehicle for analysis and refining science teaching. Mentoring is also an important way to help teachers progress by addressing their interests and concerns directly in relation to their classroom. Use the chapters on guided discussion and mentoring to plan this stage of your professional development program.

Getting Started

The time you spend preparing will contribute to the success of your professional development events. Here we describe the special things you can do to prepare for the workshops. Follow these steps as you get ready:

1. Become familiar with the teacher's and trainer's guides.

2. Find a location for the workshops.

3. Prepare to be an instructor.

STEP 1: BECOME FAMILIAR WITH THE TEACHER'S AND TRAINER'S GUIDES

A clear understanding of the curriculum and its science content will be essential if you are to help others understand this approach to teaching and learning. Carefully read the teacher's guide, familiarizing yourself with its approach and structure. Consider what aspects of this approach will be familiar to teachers and which ones will be new. Identify the parts of the guide that will be particularly helpful to teachers. Reading the guide more than once will help you build your own understanding of this teaching method and the various ways the guide supports teacher adoption.

Next, familiarize yourself with these professional development materials. Quickly reading the whole package will give you the big picture—an overview of the structure and content of the instructions and the supporting materials. In a more focused read, examine each aspect of the instructional approach and anticipate how teachers might respond.

Step 2: Find a Location for the Workshops

Select sites for your workshops that will be comfortable for indoor work and that offer a rich variety of plants and animals outdoors. If you need to create a compost heap that will encourage new animal life, do this at least two weeks in advance. See the "Essential Information" section of the teacher's guide (p. 121) for instructions.

Round or rectangular tables will provide a good surface for the indoor explorations in the basic workshops. Easy availability of an overhead projector, screen, VCR, and monitor will make your work easier.

Step 3: Prepare to Be an Instructor

Familiarity with both content and process of the workshops will give you confidence as a presenter. Take the time to complete these tasks.

- Engage in an outdoor exploration using the guidance in basic workshop 1 and in the "Getting Ready" section of the teacher's guide (p. 13). In addition, do the indoor explorations that are described in basic workshops 4 and 6.

- Think through the discussion questions, answering them for yourself. Try to anticipate how teachers will react and then imagine your responses.

- Preview the video vignettes that you will be showing. As you watch, think about the purpose of the vignettes, children's engagement with science, the science teaching strategies they illustrate, and what you want teachers to gain from the viewing and conversation.

- Collect the materials. You will need a variety of materials to facilitate the explorations. Plants, mealworms, and hand lenses are just a few. Review this list early (see the section on advance preparation for each workshop) and make plans for how you will get all of these things before the day of the workshop. Suggestions for finding many of these items can be found in the "Resources" section in the teacher's guide (p. 129).

- Prepare the handouts and overheads. For the most part, you will refer participants to resources in the teacher's guide, but there are a few handouts in the professional development package that provide guidance for small group work or observation of videos. These handouts appear at the end of the instructions for each workshop. Each participant will need a copy of each handout. The final handout is an evaluation that all participants should complete at the end of the basic or advanced workshops. The overheads, found at the end of both workshop sections, give the content a visual aid. You will need to copy them onto transparencies.

- Consider how you want to handle the "Read and Reflect" pre-assignments, which have been included for each of the basic workshops. You will need to copy and distribute them to teachers at least a week before each session. These assignments include readings in the teacher's guide and reflection questions. Completing the assignments will ensure that teachers are familiar with the content of each session and ready to participate fully in the discussions. You will probably want to collect teachers' responses and review their reflections to gain insight into teachers' understandings. This will help you tailor sessions to meet the needs of individual teachers.

- Review key instructional strategies in the resources, which will help you effectively use the various teaching strategies in these workshops.

basic workshops

The six workshops are designed to familiarize teachers with the teacher's guide and the underlying science content. They include the following:

- Workshop 1: Introduction to *Discovering Nature with Young Children*—Teachers learn about the science content and inquiry skills at the heart of *Discovering Nature with Young Children.*

- Workshop 2: Getting Ready—Teachers prepare a science-rich environment for children's indoor and outdoor explorations of plants and animals.

- Workshop 3: Overview of Open Exploration—Teachers assess their classroom environments and are introduced to the purpose and flow of open exploration.

- Workshop 4: Focused Exploration of Animals—Teachers deepen their understanding of key science concepts and inquiry skills, as well as this approach to teaching and learning, through a hands-on exploration of mealworms.

- Workshop 5: Overview of Focused Exploration—Teachers are introduced to the purpose and flow of focused exploration, and share their own classroom observations.

- Workshop 6: Focused Exploration of Plants—Teachers engage in a hands-on exploration of plants, which models ways they can encourage close observation and reflection of living things.

Each workshop includes the following sections:

- At a Glance—purpose, activities, timeline, materials, and pre-assignment for each session

- Objectives—what you want teachers to gain by the end of the session

- Overview—activity descriptions and suggestions for time management

- Instructor Preparation—materials needed and steps to take to get ready for each session

- Detailed step-by-step instructions

- Handouts to copy for each teacher

- Overheads to copy as transparencies before each session

- "Read and Reflect" pre-assignments to copy and distribute at least a week before each session

You can also refer to the key instructional strategies in "Resources" (see p. 191) to help you prepare and conduct the basic workshops.

BASIC WORKSHOP 1

Introduction to
Discovering Nature with Young Children

AT A GLANCE

Purpose:

- Gain beginning understanding of this approach to teaching and learning in the early childhood classroom.
- Begin to understand the science concepts and inquiry skills.
- Learn about the teacher's guide and how it is organized.

Activity	Time: 3 hours	Materials
Introduction Introduce your teachers to the basic workshops and the teacher's guide. Use a video vignette to show the program "in action." Invite teachers to share any previous experiences with nature.	50 minutes	• Handouts: agenda, "Read and Reflect 1" • Copies of *Discovering Nature with Young Children* teacher's guides • Self-adhesive note pads • VCR, monitor, and video cued to vignette 1 • Overhead projector, screen, and overheads 1.1–1.3
Outdoor Exploration Facilitate an outdoor naturalist exploration. Model the role that teachers will play with children by encouraging engagement with living things and focusing on interesting data.	1 hour 20 minutes	• Hand trowels, one per 3–4 participants • Hand lenses, one per 3–4 participants • Field guides, one per 3–4 participants • Clipboards, paper, and pencils, one per participant • Charts: "What We Think We'll Find Outside/Where We Think We'll Find It," "What We Found/Where We Found It," "We Wonder . . . ," and "Effective Science Teaching Strategies" • Camera and film or digital camera (optional)
The Science Introduce the science concepts and inquiry process, and help your teachers connect them to their own outdoor exploration.	50 minutes	• Overhead projector, screen, overheads 1.2 and 1.3 • "Read and Reflect 2"

Pre-assignment: Read introduction to *Discovering Nature with Young Children* and excerpts from a teacher's journal, and respond to reflection questions.

Basic Workshop 1: Introduction

OBJECTIVES

- Gain beginning understanding of this approach to teaching and learning in the early childhood classroom.

- Begin to understand the science concepts and inquiry skills.

- Learn about the teacher's guide and how it is organized.

OVERVIEW

- Introduction (50 minutes)

- Outdoor exploration (1 hour and 20 minutes)

- The science (50 minutes)

INSTRUCTOR PREPARATION

- **DISTRIBUTE "READ AND REFLECT 1"** with the teacher's guide at least one week before the workshop. Ask teachers to complete the assignment before the first workshop.

- **PREPARE AN AGENDA** that outlines the six basic workshops, as well as when and where they will take place.

- **SELECT AN OUTDOOR SITE FOR TEACHERS TO EXPLORE.** Be sure that you have selected an outdoor site that contains a variety of plants and animals. Explore it yourself so you know where and how to guide your teachers. Your time will be limited so you will want to be sure teachers are able to observe interesting plants and animals and generate and pursue questions. Create a compost pile to attract interesting small animals if you can. You should plan to do this at least two weeks in advance, using the guidelines (p. 122) in *Discovering Nature with Young Children* teacher's guide. Make plans for a rain date.

- **REVIEW STEP 1 OF OPEN EXPLORATION IN THE TEACHER'S GUIDE** in preparation for facilitating the exploration. The exploration will model the approach described in this step.

- **PREVIEW VIDEO VIGNETTE 1.** As you look at the video find the teacher and child actions that exemplify the points you want to make about this approach. The instructions that follow provide suggestions.

MATERIALS

- Handouts: agenda, "Read and Reflect" 1 and 2

- *Discovering Nature with Young Children* teacher's guides for each teacher

- Small self-adhesive note pads for each teacher

- Hand trowels and hand lenses for outdoor exploration (at least one of each per small group)

- Clipboards, paper, and pencils (one for each teacher to use during outdoor exploration)

- Video cued to vignette 1, VCR, and monitor

- Overhead projector, screen, and overheads 1.1–1.3

- Charts: "What We Think We'll Find Outside/Where We Think We'll Find It," "What We Found/Where We Found It," "We Wonder . . . ," and "Effective Science Teaching Strategies"
- Markers
- Camera and film or digital camera (optional)

Activity

INTRODUCTION (50 MINUTES)

PURPOSE:

- To set the stage by introducing the curriculum, its vision for science teaching and learning, and the nature of the work teachers will be doing with you during the workshops
- To uncover what teachers already know about the natural world and the kinds of experiences they have had, building their confidence as naturalists

1. **GIVE A SHORT PRESENTATION** (5 minutes) that provides your teachers with a brief overview of the workshops. Distribute the agenda and review it with your teachers, being explicit about any requirements for their participation in the workshops and use of the curriculum. Tell them they will be learning the following:

   - How to use *Discovering Nature with Young Children* teacher's guide to explore the native plants and animals over time with children

   - Science concepts and inquiry skills intrinsic to naturalists' work

   - The teacher's role in facilitating children's inquiry and science learning

2. **INTRODUCE THE TEACHER'S GUIDE AND THE "READ AND REFLECT" ASSIGNMENTS** (5 minutes). Tell teachers that the guide provides information and direction for conducting an investigation of the plants and animals in the immediate environment, which can take place off and on over the course of a year. Mention that the read and reflect assignments are meant to introduce them to the teacher's guide and can be used to prepare for each workshop. Explain that you will refer them back to sections of the guide during the session and suggest that they use the self-adhesive notes to mark pages that are discussed for easy reference.

3. **USE VIGNETTE 1 TO INTRODUCE *DISCOVERING NATURE WITH YOUNG CHILDREN*** (30 minutes).

   a. Begin by using overhead 1.1 to review the guiding principles listed in the introduction. Suggest that teachers look for these things as they watch the video.

> **OVERHEAD 1.1: *DISCOVERING NATURE WITH YOUNG CHILDREN* GUIDING PRINCIPLES**
>
> • All three- to five-year-olds can successfully experience rich, in-depth scientific inquiry.
>
> • The science content draws from children's experiences, is interesting and engaging, and can be explored directly and deeply over time.
>
> • Expectations are developmentally appropriate; that is, they are realistic and can be tailored to the strengths, interests, and needs of individual children.
>
> • Discussion, expression, and representation are critical ways in which children reflect on and develop theories from their active work.
>
> • Children learn from one another
>
> • Teachers take on specific roles to actively support and guide children's science learning.

b. Introduce the vignette by saying that three Head Start classrooms from Boston are shown. The children are all three- and four-year-olds, who are engaged in an exploration of nature. The sequences show varied points in time, in both indoor and outdoor exploration.

c. Ask for reactions using these questions: "Did you see anything that reminded you of a guiding principle? What did you see and which principle did it exemplify?" You might also want to discuss how the teachers in the vignette compare to teachers A, B, and C in the introduction to the teacher's guide. Ask for specifics.

Make these points about the vignette and this approach to teaching and learning:

• The children seem engaged and excited about exploring plants and animals.

• Direct experience in the immediate world is key to engagement and learning.

• Children are able to engage at varied levels of ability.

• Interactions in which children share their observations and represent their thinking are an important way to make meaning of experiences.

• The teacher is key in the process of engaging in inquiry and using experiences to gain a deeper understanding of science ideas.

When discussing how the teachers in the vignette compare to teacher C, be sure to highlight the following:

• They are building on children's enthusiasm about plants and animals.

• In all settings, the teachers understand that science learning happens over time.

• Outdoor exploration is valued, and indoor experiences take the needs of the living things into account.

• Hands-on experiences combined with dialogue and representation promote learning key science concepts.

• The teachers guide inquiry, bringing children's questions forward, encouraging close observation and representation, and helping with data collection and analysis.

d. Discuss teachers' previous experiences with nature for about ten minutes to help them understand the science that is intrinsic to naturalist work. Encourage a few people to talk about outdoor experiences they have had that focused on living things. You might want to start the conversation by sharing a brief story of your own and then asking some questions. If you do tell a story of your own, choose one to which you think teachers can relate, one that might help them make connections to their own life.

Use the following questions to guide the discussion:

- What kinds of places do you go where there are living things?

- What kinds of plants and animals have you seen?

- Are any of you bird-watchers? Gardeners? Hikers? What have you noticed/learned from these experiences?

- What questions do you have about the life of a living thing?

- Have any of you used binoculars, hand lenses, or other tools?

> It is important for learners to talk about what they already know. Making the connections to their knowledge and past experiences acknowledges their value and helps them integrate new information. In this case, it can ease them into science by helping them realize science is already a part of their lives.
>
> A number of people enjoy bird-watching and probably use binoculars and field guides as they look for birds in their own backyards. Some might have used them on a whale watch or trip to protect sea turtles as they lay their eggs. Others may walk or hike, stopping to look for particular plants or vernal pools and document what they see in a notebook or with a camera. Some might collect seashells, using guides to help them identify the animals from which the shells came. And still others may raise houseplants, vegetables, fish, or feed birds outside their window.

OUTDOOR EXPLORATION (1 HOUR 20 MINUTES)

PURPOSE: Through the process of engaging teachers in an outdoor exploration you will achieve the following:

- Provide a beginning experience with inquiry and the science content on which you will build throughout the workshops

- Reinforce the importance of going outdoors to see living things in their natural environment

- Model the teacher's role in facilitating scientific explorations

- Model a science talk that helps teachers build on one another's understanding in the same way children can

1. **INTRODUCE THE OUTDOOR EXPERIENCE WITH A CHART** (10 minutes) by saying that they will be engaging in an outdoor exploration of the kind they will facilitate for children—however, this particular experience is designed for adults. Tell them that you will be modeling the kinds of interactions that they will be asked to use when they implement the teacher's guide. Show teachers the naturalist tools, then help them think about the plants and animals they might find and where they might find them.

   Ask a few questions, such as the following:

   - What living things do you think we'll see when we go out?

   - Where do you think we will find plants? Animals?

List responses on the chart, "What We Think We'll Find Outside/Where We Think We'll Find Them." As teachers make these comments, ask them questions, such as the following:

- Why do you think we'll find those plants? Animals?

- Have you seen them before? Where?

- Do you always see them on tree bark? Might they be somewhere else? Why do you think so?

> These questions help people realize and make explicit their own learning strategies as well as the many ways in which knowledge is acquired, such as books, experiences, or other people.

2. **GIVE INSTRUCTIONS** (5 minutes) for the exploration. Ask your teachers to form groups of three or four. Explain that you are all going outdoors to get a sense of the living things that can be found and investigated in the immediate environment. Ask them to look for living things: plants and animals. Ask them to consider the questions that arise as they find, observe, and think about plants and animals. Tell them to use their clipboards, paper, and pencils to sketch one or two of the plants and animals they find that are particularly interesting, and jot down ideas and questions they have. Let them know that they will have forty-five minutes (this assumes five minutes to get out and five minutes to return) to do this exploration.

> Some of the teachers may have trouble with the idea of looking for insects outdoors. Tell them they just need to observe; they don't have to touch anything.

Remind people to try to pay attention to the kinds of interactions you are having with them, as you will be modeling some strategies that can be applied to their own teaching, even though their responses are likely to differ from those of their children.

3. **HELP TEACHERS GET STARTED** (25 minutes). Encourage them to look carefully at the plants and animals they see, and to look in places they might not have thought to look, such as under rocks and leaves, in a pile of debris, on and under a tree or an old box, or on branches. Ask questions that encourage them to describe what they observe and help them make connections and inquire more deeply about what they are observing and thinking about. Focus your questions and discussions around the science concepts and inquiry skills.

It is important to use the science concepts when focusing teachers' exploration so they come away with interesting experiences and data. Ask what they are noticing about the living things they find. Call attention to physical characteristics and/or behavior. Wonder why living things are under a log or in a tree. This is an important learning experience that they will build on as the science becomes more explicit. The related science content and inquiry skills are in parentheses.

- What are the primary physical characteristics of this organism? (Characteristics of living things; observation)

- What behaviors can you observe? (Characteristics of living things; observation)

- Where did you find this plant or animal? (Habitat; observation)

- What are the characteristics of the location? (Habitat; needs; observation)

- Why do you think you found the plant or animal in that particular location? (Needs; analysis)

- What do you think the plant or animal needs to survive? What do you notice that leads you to say that? (Basic needs; analysis)

- Are there other places we might find this plant or animal? (Habitat and basic needs; developing relationships; making predictions)

- What structures of the plant or animal seem to help it survive in that particular location? (Physical characteristics; adaptation; analysis)

Use the question "Why do you think so?" regularly. It will help teachers reflect on how they know what they know.

Acknowledge their findings and help them find appropriate places to look. Encourage teachers to sketch one or two of the living things and jot some notes, such as where they were found, how they seem to move, their coloring, and so on. Also encourage them to jot down questions they have.

4. **HELP THE TEACHERS IDENTIFY QUESTIONS** (20 minutes) to explore. After the initial period of observation and discovery, help each group identify a question to pursue and a plan for their inquiry. The emphasis here is on questions the groups will be able to investigate by gathering evidence in a short time frame. When questions are generated, ask, "How could you find that out?" For those who are not generating their own questions, model a process for doing so by saying something like, "I wonder where the ant is taking that crumb of bread?" Or, "Do you wonder how many different kinds of plants we can find in our yard?"

Teachers may want to explore questions like these:

- How does this animal move?

- Is this plant a home or food for any particular animal?

- Which locations seem to have the most diversity of living things? What are some key characteristics of those locations?

- What interrelationships might exist between the plants and animals in a particular location?

Allow about fifteen to twenty minutes for the teachers to complete these investigations and then ask them to return to the classroom. Be sure you leave time for the fifteen-minute science talk back in the classroom.

5. **BRING THE TEACHERS TOGETHER FOR A FIFTEEN-MINUTE SCIENCE TALK.** Facilitate a reflective discussion about your teachers' outdoor experiences. List their ideas on the chart,

"What We Found/Where We Found It." Ask your teachers to look at their notes and drawings and share some of the things they learned and the questions they raised. Use openended questions to help teachers focus on the different living things they found, how they are alike and similar in terms of their characteristics, their behaviors, and the habitats in which they live.

During the science talk, help teachers compare what they actually found with what they predicted they would find during your introduction to their outdoor experience.

An example of probing questions:

"You found a beetle? . . . Where did you find it? . . . Why did you decide to look there? . . . Why do you think the beetle was in that location?"

6. **DISCUSS HOW THE TEACHERS' OWN EXPERIENCES ARE LIKELY TO BE DIFFERENT** from those of children (5 minutes) as well as similar. Include the following points:

   Differences

   - Adults generally bring much more prior knowledge (although not always the correct information) to this kind of experience.

   - Adults generally have longer attention spans.

   - Children are often more willing to touch things and get their hands dirty.

   Similarities

   - The focus for both is on observing and describing plants and animals—not simply naming and explaining.

   - You might not have thought of where to look (under rocks/leaves), and were excited to find living things—kids usually respond that way too.

THE SCIENCE (50 MINUTES)

PURPOSE: Inquiry is a concept that is central to science and should be a part of all science education. Therefore, one of the teacher's primary goals is to help children experience and use the processes of inquiry, integrating them into their daily experiences. It is also key to the teaching approach. The science content is also an important feature of *Discovering Nature with Young Children*. It is central to every naturalist experience and conversation. The inquiry and content are introduced here and will be reinforced throughout the workshops.

1. **INTRODUCE THE CONCEPT OF INQUIRY** (10 minutes). Tell teachers that they have been engaged in a part of the process of inquiry and that it is a central idea in science and *Discovering Nature with Young Children*. Refer them to the inquiry diagram on p. 116 of the teacher's guide as you show overhead 1.2: Inquiry diagram. Make the following points as you talk about the diagram.

   - *It is a dynamic process.*
     This process is cyclical in nature. It cannot be fully represented in a linear two-dimensional diagram.

- *It begins with engagement and wondering.*
  Experience with things, materials, and events is the basis of inquiry. This is a time for play. At this point, the teachers and children are noticing different organisms, what they look like, and how they behave. You may wonder about many things: where living things are, why they look the way they do, if you've seen them before, how they move or eat, and so on.

- *Wondering leads to more focused observation and questions.*
  As you explore, you may have lots of questions. Why are all these beetles under the log? Where is the worm's mouth? Some people ask their questions; others may reveal their questions through actions, such as exploring the ground beneath the log to find out why it is so inviting to beetles.

- *Questions focus observation and lead to investigation.*
  In order to pursue something in depth, a single question needs to be identified and refined. There are many kinds of questions. At this point, you and the children need to consider which questions can be answered through simple investigations or which can be modified and pursued through investigation. Ask predicting questions, such as "What will happen if . . ."

- *Investigation is a cyclical process.*
  Investigations begin with a focus or question: How do snails move? How are leaves the same and how are they different? They involve planning, observing closely, recording experiences, and reflecting in order to identify patterns and construct theories and explanations. New questions arise and are pursued. With your guidance, the children can engage in this experimental stage of inquiry.

- *Share, discuss, reflect, and draw conclusions.*
  This is a time for making meaning of investigations. In small and large groups, you and the children share and form simple theories and generalizations that will deepen your understanding of the concepts being explored.

2. **REFLECT ON THE ROLE INQUIRY PLAYED IN THEIR EXPLORATION** (15 minutes). Ask teachers what aspects of the diagram describe experiences they had during the exploration. Here are some guiding questions:

- How would you describe the inquiry you just engaged in? Did you experience particular aspects of the diagram during your exploration? What are they?

- Which questions drove your investigation?

- What kind of data did you collect related to your questions? How did you document the data?

Now help them think more analytically about their inquiry:

- Did identifying questions play a role in your investigation? What role did it play?

- How did you use the data you collected? (Ask for specifics and about insights they might have had as they documented.)

- What evidence influenced you to change your thinking?

- When and how did you draw some conclusions?

As you make specific connections between their activity and the diagram, emphasize the following:

- Questions and focused activity grow out of an early period of engagement called open exploration.

- Questions help focus observation and investigation.

- Sharing ideas exposes one to more data and to different perspectives and ideas, and opens new doors for investigation.

- Recording data as it is collected is useful because it provides a reference for analysis.

- Science is grounded in evidence. Inquiry is about finding the evidence.

3. **INTRODUCE THE SCIENCE CONCEPTS** (25 minutes) by saying that your questions and comments during their exploration were designed to focus them on particular science concepts. Refer them to descriptions of the science concepts that appear in "Getting Ready" on p. 13 of the teacher's guide. Suggest marking the page with a self-adhesive note for quick reference. Review overhead 1.3.

OVERHEAD 1.3: SCIENCE CONCEPTS

- **Characteristics of living things**
  Living things have a number of basic characteristics that are easily observable, such as color, size, and structure. Noticing these characteristics can lead children to wonder more deeply, for example about how a cricket's color might help it survive, or why an oak tree might have so many acorns.

- **Living and nonliving**
  All things on earth are either living or nonliving. Living things share certain characteristics (for instance, they grow and reproduce) that will become more evident to children as they acquire experience. Children have common misunderstandings, such as that to be alive something must move. Thus plants do not appear to be living to children, while cars might be considered alive.

- **Needs of living things**
  Living things must have certain needs met if they are to survive, grow, develop, and reproduce. Animals need food, water, air, and a space in which to live. Plants need light, water, air, and space in which to grow.

- **Life cycle**
  All living things have a life cycle that includes a beginning (birth for animals, germination for plants), growth, development, and death. All living things also reproduce, creating a cycle that maintains the species.

- **Diversity and variation**
  There is tremendous diversity of plant and animal species on earth. In a vacant lot you might see spiders, ants, pill bugs, grasses, weeds, bushes, and so on. Within each kind of living thing you will see variation. For instance, not all worms, snails, or oak trees are exactly the same.

- **Habitat**
  The habitat is the part of the total environment that a particular living thing uses to meet all its basic needs. For example, a worm's habitat can be a small patch of earth, while a rabbit will need enough space in order to find plants to eat and places in which to hide from predators. Each of these habitats provides for all of the worm's or rabbit's needs.

Encourage teachers to generate an example of how they may have encountered each science concept during their outdoor exploration. In their brief experience, they are likely not to have touched on all of these concepts, but you can look for the following:

- Descriptions of the characteristics of plants and animals they found, including physical descriptions and any behaviors (such as movement) they may have observed

- Mention of the diversity and variation of organisms

- Observations that might have related to the needs of outdoor organisms

- Experiences with living and nonliving

4. **CONCLUDE THE WORKSHOP** by telling teachers that they will have more opportunities to engage in and talk about inquiry, the science concepts, and the teaching approach in future workshops. You might want to collect "Read and Reflect 1" to get a better understanding of what teachers are thinking. Thank teachers for their participation. Give them "Read and Reflect 2" and confirm the time and place for the next workshop.

READ AND REFLECT 1: INTRODUCTION TO *DISCOVERING NATURE WITH YOUNG CHILDREN*

Name: _____

Before coming to workshop 1, read the introduction to the teacher's guide and the excerpts from a teacher's journal. Respond to these questions as you reflect on what you read. This information will be helpful in the workshop discussion.

1. As you read about teachers A, B, and C, did you make connections to your own teaching? Which teacher was most like you?

2. What were the similarities?

3. What challenges will you face in learning the approach of teacher C?

READ AND REFLECT 2:
GETTING READY

Name: _____

Before coming to workshop 2, read "Getting Ready" and "Essential Information," as well as the "Books and Media" sections in "Resources" at the back of the teacher's guide. Copy and complete the discovering nature environment checklist in the appendices. Once it is complete, reflect on the following questions. This information will be helpful in the workshop discussion.

1. What are the strengths of your environment? What important elements do you have for your exploration of nature?

2. What challenges do you face? What important elements are you missing?

Getting Ready

AT A GLANCE

Purpose:

- Gain understanding of the important elements of a science-rich learning environment
- Prepare for indoor and outdoor explorations of nature

Activity	Time: 1.5 hours	Materials
Using the Outdoor Environment Emphasize the importance of the outdoor environment as you discuss the spaces teachers have available. Help them develop strategies for dealing with management issues related to working with children outdoors.	30 minutes	• Chart: "Our Outdoor Environment"
Preparing the Indoor Environment Discuss important elements of an environment that encourages an exploration of nature using photos for analysis. Guide teachers as they prepare terraria for their classrooms and plant a variety of seeds in preparation for workshop 6.	1 hour	• Overhead projector, screen, and overheads 2.1–2.4 • Chart: "Creating a Science Rich Environment" • Clear plastic containers • Gravel, charcoal, and soil • Plants • Seeds, soil, cups, paper towels, clear plastic bottles, carrot tops, bulbs • Copies of "Read and Reflect 3"

Pre-assignment: Read "Getting Ready" and complete the "Classroom Environment Checklist" on p. 139 of the teacher's guide. Complete reflection questions.

Basic Workshop 2: Getting Ready

OBJECTIVES

- Gain understanding of the important elements of a science-rich learning environment
- Prepare for indoor and outdoor explorations of nature

OVERVIEW

- Using the outdoor environment (30 minutes)
- Preparing the indoor environment (1 hour)

INSTRUCTOR PREPARATION

- **COLLECT TERRARIUM MATERIALS.** In preparing for the terrarium activity, see the section on constructing a terrarium that appears on p. 123 of the *Discovering Nature with Young Children* teacher's guide. You will need to dig up some plants along with the soil and small animals (such as worms, beetles, and so on) the day before the session and place them in a large container. Teachers will use these materials to construct a number of small terraria.

- **PREPARE FOR STARTING INDOOR PLANTS.** To prepare for the indoor planting, see the section on growing plants that appears on p. 127 of the teacher's guide. Be sure to make provisions for care of the plants until workshop 6. Ideally, they can be placed where teachers can observe and document their growth.

MATERIALS

- Overhead projector, screen, and overheads 2.1–2.4
- Copies of "Read and Reflect 3"
- Clear plastic container, with cover, for each group of four
- Gravel or sand, charcoal, and soil for each group of four
- Plants for each group of four
- Materials for starting indoor plants for each group of four: at least two different varieties of seeds, including beans; soil; cups; paper towels; one- or two-liter clear plastic bottles; carrot tops; bulbs (garlic or narcissus)
- Charts: "Our Outdoor Environment" (with three columns: "Space," "What We Found," and "Where We Found It") and "Creating a Science-Rich Environment"

Activity

USING THE OUTDOOR ENVIRONMENT (25 MINUTES)

PURPOSE: Outdoor exploration is an essential experience for young children who are discovering nature. Teachers are often working in places where it is hard to find a usable outdoor space.

It is important to help them develop strategies for using the spaces available to them as a way of emphasizing the importance of outdoor exploration.

1. **DISCUSS CHARACTERISTICS OF THE OUTDOOR ENVIRONMENT** (10 minutes). Suggest teachers think back on the exploration they did in workshop 1 and on the possibility of going out with children. Ask them what conditions they think are essential to a successful outdoor exploration of nature.

    Look for the following topics:

    - There are a variety of plants like flowers, weeds, bushes, and trees.

    - Small animals such as snails, ants, pill bugs, or worms are easily found.

    - Larger animals like birds and squirrels can be observed.

    - The area is near the classroom.

    - There are other areas of interest for distractible children (playground, open space to run around, and so on).

    - The area is safe for children.

    - The area is accessible to all children.

    You will want to probe for specifics, revealing just what teachers know about exploring nature outdoors. Ask questions such as the following:

    - *Where are we likely to find plants and small animals?*
      You want to be sure they have access to a variety of types of plants and animals to explore in the focused exploration. Ideally, this includes trees, other smaller plants, and small and larger animals. Help them discover that shady areas with dead leaves, rotting logs, or stones on the ground attract small animals.

    - *Why might a tree be a good thing to have?*
      Not only does the focused exploration allow one to observe a tree over time, but trees provide a rich habitat for animal life. It is possible to find birds or squirrels, as well as ants, caterpillars, or other insects.

    - *What would make the area safe for children?*
      You might want to talk about physical barriers that protect them from traffic and about the removal of any poisonous or thorny plants or glass. They might also want to check with families about allergies their children might have.

2. **DISCUSS TEACHERS' ASSESSMENT OF AVAILABLE OUTDOOR AREAS** (20 minutes). Ask teachers to report on what they found when they were completing the outdoor section of the environment checklist for their homework. List on the chart you prepared, "Our Outdoor Environment," the places that they investigated and what they found where. For example, if one of the sites is the playground, write "playground," what they found there, and where on the playground they found it. See the following example:

CHART EXAMPLE

Location	What We Found
Paved playground—under trees in north corner	• Anthill at foot of one tree • 3 trees • 1 bird nest • Worms near surface when we dug under the dead leaves
Paved playground—old pavement has cracks	• Ants • Weeds

After completing the list, ask teachers if they have enough places to investigate with the children. If they aren't satisfied, do some problem solving with them. Consider the following:

- Make a compost pile. See p. 122 of the teacher's guide for instructions. Be sure teachers understand that they should make a compost pile at least two weeks in advance.

- Recruit volunteers who can help a teacher take small groups to a neighborhood field or park.

- Place large tubs in the outdoor space and put plants in them.

PREPARING THE INDOOR ENVIRONMENT (1 HOUR)

PURPOSE: The indoor environment is also important when exploring nature. Plants and animals can be studied closely over time in temporary habitats created by the children. This activity will address some of the key elements of an indoor environment, and provide ideas for teachers' own classrooms. Many teachers will not have done this kind of preparation before. Working together they can prepare a terrarium for their classroom, as well as plant seeds for workshop 6.

1. **INTRODUCE THE TOPIC OF INDOOR ENVIRONMENTS** (5 minutes). Tell teachers that indoor experiences will complement children's outdoor explorations. These indoor experiences allow children to observe organisms more closely and help children begin to think about living things' needs in such a way that they can then care for them indoors. Draw on their past experience by asking, "I imagine many of you already encourage this kind of exploration. What kinds of indoor setups for living things do you have?" "How have you encouraged interest in living things through use of your environment?" Listen to responses on the chart you prepared, "Creating a Science-Rich Environment." Don't spend more than five minutes on this conversation.

2. DISCUSS CREATING AN ENVIRONMENT THAT ENCOURAGES EXPLORATION OF NATURE (30 minutes) using overheads 2.1–2.4. There are two ways you can do this activity.

- If you have time, print the overheads on paper and place each on a piece of newsprint. Mount these around the room and ask your teachers in teams to write on each chart how this particular environment encourages inquiry. After fifteen minutes, bring the teachers together and read the responses at each chart. Add important ideas to the chart you have started.

- If you are running behind schedule, use the overheads as overheads and discuss each as you project it, getting ideas about the photo from your teachers and adding important ideas that aren't mentioned.

OVERHEAD 2.1:

How does this environment encourage exploration of nature?

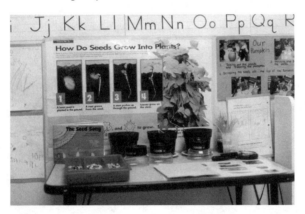

Note: All materials at a child eye level—children's work, posters, reference books, magnifying glasses, a poster of children's experience, the alphabet

OVERHEAD 2.2:

How does this environment encourage exploration of nature?

Note: Terrarium at table with access from multiple sides, reference books

OVERHEAD 2.3:

How does this environment encourage exploration of nature?

Note: Wall display using multimedia to tell story of a tree children are observing, bin of related books

OVERHEAD 2.4:

How does this environment encourage exploration of nature?

Note: Paper is on a clipboard, allowing for easy use outdoors. Children have easy access to everything they need to complete observational sketches.

Be sure to mention these points:

- Displays are at children's eye level.
- Displays address children's recent interests and include their work.
- Relevant books are within reach where naturalists are working.
- Magnifying glasses and penlights are accessible.
- Commonly used vocabulary words are on cards where children can see them.
- Varied representation materials are available.
- Plants and other living things are in safe places.
- Terrarium is placed on tables with observation places on all sides during choice time.

3. Make terrariums and plant seeds (25 minutes).

    a. Tell teachers that they are now going to learn how to assemble a terrarium. Explain that terraria are an essential aspect of open and focused exploration: they provide a natural habitat for visiting animals, allowing for close observation in the classroom. Show teachers the available materials and refer them to the section in essential information (pp. 123–125) in the teacher's guide. Ask them to form groups of four and follow the written directions. As teachers are constructing their terraria, you should wander from group to group offering advice and answering questions.

    b. Refer teachers to the section of resources about growing and caring for plants, and tell them that they will now begin some indoor plants that they will observe in workshop 6. Ask them to form groups of four and follow the written directions. As with the terraria, you should wander from group to group answering questions.

    c. Each group of four should be sure to start *at least* one bulb, one set of germinating bean seeds out of soil, and one carrot or beet top. Starting other plants will add to the richness of the exploration of plants in workshop 6.

4. In conclusion, tell teachers that you will discuss their "Classroom Environment Checklists" (p. 139 in the teacher's guide) in the next workshop. You might want to collect "Read and Reflect 2" in order to better understand their environment issues. Distribute "Read and Reflect 3" and confirm the time and place of the next workshop.

READ AND REFLECT 3:
OPEN EXPLORATION

Name: _____

Before coming to workshop 3, read the open exploration and science teaching sections in the teacher's guide. Respond to these questions as you reflect on what you read. This information will be helpful in the workshop discussion.

We will talk about the following four purposes of open exploration. What examples of these can you find in the open exploration steps? Be specific and note the page numbers of your references.

1. Introduces the children to living things. How exactly does open exploration do this?

2. Introduces role and tools of the naturalist. When and how does open exploration do this?

3. Helps children learn to use indoor and outdoor environments. What are four specific strategies suggested to help children learn to use indoor and outdoor environments? Refer to the teacher's role in "Resources" as well as to open exploration.

4. Begins to engage in inquiry. In what steps are the children engaged in inquiry? What inquiry skills are they developing at this point?

You should also answer these questions:

- How do you imagine involving families in these explorations? What will the benefit be to you and to the children?
- What challenges will you face as you implement open exploration for the first time?

Overview of Open Exploration

AT A GLANCE

Purpose:
- Become familiar with open exploration, its purpose, and the cycle of activity
- Gain basic understanding of the teacher's role during open exploration
- Begin to understand how children might engage in open exploration
- Discuss needs of own environment and plan for adaptations

Activity	Time: 1.5 hours	Materials
Overview of Open Exploration Introduce the purpose and flow of open exploration and help teachers connect this information to their exploration from workshop 1. Use vignette to illustrate child engagement and the teacher's role.	1 hour	• Overhead projector, screen, and overheads 3.1 and 3.2 • VCR, monitor, and video cued to vignette 2 • Copies of the vignette observation form and transcript to video vignette 2
Preparing Your Own Environment Support teachers as they discuss their assessment of their own classroom environments, available tools, and use of time.	30 minutes	• Copies of "Read and Reflect 4"

Pre-assignment: Read "Open Exploration," "Observation and Assessment," and "Involving Families" in the teacher's guide and complete reflection questions.

Basic Workshop 3: Overview of Open Exploration

OBJECTIVES

- Become familiar with open exploration, its purpose, and the cycle of activity
- Gain basic understanding of the teacher's role during open exploration
- Begin to understand how children might engage in open exploration
- Assess needs of own environment and plan for adaptations

OVERVIEW

- Overview of open exploration (45 minutes)
- Preparing your own environment (45 minutes)

INSTRUCTOR PREPARATION

- **PREVIEW VIGNETTE 2** and identify the points you want to make during the discussion. Refer to the following video instructions.
- **REMIND TEACHERS TO BRING THEIR "CLASSROOM ENVIRONMENT CHECKLISTS."**

MATERIALS

- Overhead projector, screen, and overheads 3.1 and 3.2
- VCR, monitor, and video cued to vignette 2
- Copies of vignette observation form, the transcript to video vignette 2, and "Read and Reflect 4"

Activity

OVERVIEW OF OPEN EXPLORATION (45 MINUTES)

PURPOSE: As teachers prepare to use open exploration, they will need to think about three aspects of the curriculum:

- The sequence of steps and types of experiences children will have
- The role of the teacher as a facilitator of science inquiry
- Young children's early engagement with the natural world

The presented material will become more meaningful to teachers when it is connected to their exploration, the teacher's guide, and the vignette.

1. **PROVIDE AN OVERVIEW OF OPEN EXPLORATION** (30 minutes) using overheads 3.1 and 3.2. Discuss the purpose of open exploration using overhead 3.1. Mention that teachers have engaged in an open exploration in workshop 1, making some connection to their experience as you talk.

OVERHEAD 3.1: PURPOSE OF OPEN EXPLORATION

- **Give children opportunities to wonder, notice, and explore.**
  Wondering, noticing, and exploring mark children's entry into inquiry. Using outdoor environment and finding and observing plants and animals in their native habitats are key to open exploration. Share questions and early theories to draw out initial observations.

- **Give children the support, materials, and time they need to begin their exploration.**
  Learning to use the tools and assuming the role of a naturalist are important aspects of open exploration. This takes time both indoors and outdoors, learning to use the important tools (hand lenses, penlights, guide books, paper, clip boards, and pens) with teacher guidance.

Ask teachers for examples of these purposes from the teacher's guide, as per the reading assignment. You might also ask what they noticed about the instructions and which features they will find especially helpful as they use the teacher's guide. Ask teachers to be specific, citing page numbers for easy reference.

This conversation is designed to help your teachers learn to navigate through the teacher's guide. The ideas of those who have taken a careful look will help those who are feeling overwhelmed. Look for answers such as these:

Introduce the children to living things:

- In step 1 children share previous experiences, look at a houseplant or bug as they talk about the term *naturalist,* go outdoors looking for plants and animals, and talk about what they saw.

- In step 2 the children continue to look at plants and animals and talk about them indoors.

- Indoor and outdoor experiences continue in steps 3–5.

Introduce the naturalist's role and tools:

- The role is introduced in step 1 during the conversation at the beginning.

- The tools are introduced in step 3.

Help children learn to use indoor and outdoor environments:

- This happens in all of the steps. Help teachers focus on the kinds of support they can provide.

- Connect the new experiences to related experiences the children have had previously.

- Establish "naturalist" rules.

- Use focusing questions as children explore.

- Document experiences and make panels for use with children.

- Encourage descriptions of what children are observing.

- Enhance observations with tools that children can use.

Children begin to engage in inquiry:

- In step 1 the children will notice plants and animals. They will describe their characteristics and locations. The teacher records the data collected and facilitates a group discussion of the items found.

- These aspects of inquiry are repeated in step 2.

- Inquiry is enriched with the use of tools in step 3.

a. Present the flow of open exploration using overhead 3.2.

Overhead 3.2: Flow of Open Exploration

- **Step 1: Introduce children to discovering nature**
  Introduce the role of the naturalist with a brief conversation with the whole group. Do a thirty-minute outdoor exploration and a ten-minute science talk.

- **Step 2: Introduce children to observing living things in an indoor terrarium**
  Again meet with the whole group and briefly introduce the terrarium (five to ten minutes). Follow this with small group observation time, four or five days a week. Place the terrarium on a table where a group of children can observe from each side. Facilitate a science talk after each observation.

- **Step 3: Teach children how to use hand lenses, penlights, and trowels**
  Introduce hand lenses and penlights in small groups, and give children a chance to use them as they continue to observe the terrarium or outdoors. Continue the introduction until all children have participated.

- **Step 4: Continue to explore and reflect**
  Repeat explorations regularly for about two weeks, giving children additional opportunities to observe indoors and outdoors. Conduct science talks after each outdoor exploration.

Make these points as you talk about open exploration:

- The guide provides detailed instructions that teachers can follow for each step.

- All children will need a period of open exploration to become familiar with the tools and the organisms.

- The children will move in and out of open exploration as they are introduced to new tools or organisms. For example, if a new animal is introduced they will openly explore before focusing on particular aspects.

- Open exploration will vary depending on the children's prior experiences and their developmental levels. Have they explored nature in preschool or at home? If so, they will need less time in open exploration— some children may take a week or two; others may take most of the exploration.

    b. Emphasize the importance of sending home the family letter in the involving families section. Also, mention the assessment and observation section. Note the value of copying the observation record and using it regularly during the exploration.

2. **Introduce vignette 2** (30 minutes). Explain that this vignette, which was filmed in a Boston Head Start, shows a small group of three- and four-year-old children exploring living things in a park. They are engaged in open exploration. The children are learning to look for animals outdoors.

    a. Distribute the transcript and the vignette observation form, and tell teachers they will use this form to take notes as they view the video, noting children's engagement and the strategies the teacher uses to encourage engagement and inquiry.

    b. Show the vignette.

    c. After the viewing, discuss observations connecting what teachers have seen to overhead 3.2: Flow of Open Exploration. Ask the following questions:

- What did you notice about the children's engagement?

- Which of the science concepts were being explored here?

- What aspects of the inquiry process were being experienced?

- What role did the teacher play?

- What connections can you make to the steps in open exploration?

Look for responses like these:

- Child engagement—The children are clearly excited about looking for and finding living things. They are moving quickly, trying varied locations, and moving on when they find something. Their interest is in variety more than looking closely at any of the animals they find.

- Relationship to science content and inquiry—The teacher is interjecting questions and comments that call attention to science concepts. For example, "Maybe you can find some animals that eat berries" (needs of living things); "Where did you find the spider?" (habitat); "I wonder if there is a caterpillar up there since there's a hole on the leaf" (habitat, needs); and "What do you think is going on in the hole, Jasmine?" (characteristics of living things). She encourages inquiry ("Where did you find your worm, Jasmine?"), records children's data, facilitates their reflection back in the classroom, helps them observe closely by putting the worm on paper, models wonder ("Wow! I wonder where he came from?").

- The teacher's role—The teacher is playing a key role in guiding this exploration. To begin, she has found a safe place for the children to explore outdoors. Her comments and questions maintain a focus on the task of finding animals, suggest important science ideas (where animals come from is important information), and encourage inquiry. She is teaching them about the work of naturalists by commenting on handling the animals gently. She is collecting the data by writing down what they find and where. This not only provides an important record for their later conversations, but it models the important literacy work that naturalists do.

- Connections to steps in *Discovering Nature with Young Children*—This is step 1, the outdoor exploration, and group sharing.

Leading group science talks is one of the hardest teacher roles. Large group talks challenge teachers to engage all of the children at the same time. Small groups are easier to manage. The challenge always is developing strategies for going deeper with the science. The teacher's guide provides guidance and has some suggestions for issues that may arise. You may also want to refer participants to the teaching section of resources.

PREPARING YOUR OWN ENVIRONMENT (30 MINUTES)

PURPOSE: This activity will help teachers translate these ideas about the environment into plans for their classroom. It will provide an opportunity to put together an order if tools, supplies, or resources are needed.

1. **IDENTIFY STRENGTHS FROM THE "CLASSROOM ENVIRONMENT CHECKLIST"**
   (10 minutes). Focus on the first three sections and ask, "What do you have to help you create a rich environment for young naturalist inquiry?" Connect teachers' resources to the chart of ideas they have made with you. Find out if any of them have things they can share or sources others should know about.

2. **Discuss environmental needs** (20 minutes). Discuss one category at a time as you review the needs they have identified and help them think about solutions. The box below has suggestions for addressing each category. Before solving problems, give other teachers a chance to share their strategies, asking, "Does anyone have a suggestion for . . . ?"

Use these questions, based on the checklist, to facilitate the conversation. Focus on helping teachers with their needs.

- Did any of you find challenges with your schedule?

- Did anyone have issues providing space for living things and displays?

- Do you all have the necessary tools?

- Do you have extra adults to help? Do you have ideas for recruiting them?

- How are you going to find appropriate children's books?

This is an opportunity to reinforce the value of materials and time in inquiry science. Pursue these issues with a focus on solving them rather than communicating that they are not important.

- **Time:** Children need ample time to experience the living world in a way that builds understanding. They need to make repeated visits to plants and animals for observation and observational drawing. They will spend longer periods with worms and snails when they are investigating behaviors such as movement. Perhaps some teachers can suggest useful strategies for dealing with time. Remember to talk about the need for longer periods of time for outdoor exploration. Remind them that it can happen during recess or another outdoor play time.

- **Space:** Children must be comfortable as they observe and represent the living things in the classroom. This requires a certain kind of available table space during choice time, as well as accessibility to observation tools and representation materials. It is also important to have space to display their work and other posters or pictures at the children's eye level that will pique their interest. Allow teachers to share strategies here. Teachers are often dealing with space constraints and some may have developed unique approaches that work for them. Sometimes it is necessary to rearrange the room for a period of time to accommodate a special focus. Help teachers think about how to find the table space that they will need to put the terrarium and plants on during choice time. Remind them that the room can always be put back together when the exploration of nature is done.

- **Tools:** Tools increase children's ability to observe the natural world and represent their ideas about it. Note that resources for purchasing tools are listed in the teacher's guide on p. 129. Most of these are inexpensive, but do need to be of good quality.

- **Adults:** Although not absolutely necessary, extra adults are a big help, especially outdoors. A letter to families (p. 131 in the teacher's guide) can often generate support and volunteers. Sometimes, however, volunteers are unavailable. Suggest teachers ask their administrator to help find an interested civic group, such as a local Audubon Society chapter or Chamber of Commerce.

- **Books:** Hopefully everyone uses the library. If not, help them locate the nearest branch. There may be other ideas for naturalist books, like a local Audubon sanctuary with a library. Be sure that books are shared. Briefly mention the importance of books and point out that an annotated list of recommended books is included on p. 130 of the teacher's guide.

---

3. **Conclude the workshop** by collecting "Read and Reflect 3." Give them "Read and Reflect 4," review your expectations, and confirm the time and place for the next workshop.

VIGNETTE OBSERVATION FORM

Note your observations by identifying the teacher strategies and child responses in separate columns.

Child Behavior/Comments	Teacher Response

TRANSCRIPT OF VIDEO VIGNETTE 2: OUTDOOR OPEN EXPLORATION

Scene 1: Five children and their teacher (also named Karen) are outdoors looking for small animals. The scene opens as they are bent down, gathered around a tree.

The children: Karen, Kevin, Jasmine, Dione, and William

Child: Look at this!

Teacher: Did you find any more animals? *(Karen holds out something in her hand.)* Oh, you found a berry. *(Kevin holds out another berry.)* That is some kind of a berry. Maybe some animals eat these. Maybe you can find some animals that might eat the berries.

Child: You know what? Squirrels, squirrels eat some leaves in the trees.

Teacher: Let's see if we can find some squirrels. Where would we find them, the squirrels?

(Dione points to a leaf on the tree.)

Dione: *(Inaudible)* caterpillar did that.

Teacher: You see a hole on a leaf. You think a caterpillar did that?

(Dione pulls leaf down and examines leaf closely.)

Teacher: I wonder if there is a caterpillar up there since there's a hole on the leaf.

Child: I can't reach up there.

(Children go to another spot on the grass.)

Teachers: Did you find an animal?

Karen: *(Cupping hands)* A spider.

Teacher: Where did you find the spider?

Jasmine: Over here.

Teacher: Show me.

(Jasmine puts the spider on her arm.)

Teacher: In the grass or in the dirt. Put it down on the paper. *(Jasmine puts it on paper.)* What kind of animal is this?

Dione: An ant.

Teacher: An ant.

William: *(Inaudible)* and I scratch all around.

Teacher: So we found another ant—in the dirt and the grass.

(Scene changes to Jasmine digging a hole in the grass and children near the concrete slab with bench. A child finds something on the concrete.)

Child: I found another ant.

Kevin: Karen, come and see. We found some red ants.

William: We found some red ants.

(Children gather around talking excitedly, but hard to understand. The teacher joins them.)

Teacher: What did you find? Little red animals?

(Children talk all together excitedly.)

Child: Down in the ground.

(A girl comes over with something in her hand.)

Child: *(Yelling)* A worm, a worm!

Teacher: Where did you find your worm, Jasmine?

Jasmine: In the big hole.

Teacher: In the big hole? In the dirt?

(Jasmine puts worm on teacher's clipboard as she is writing.)

(Children dig another hole.)

Teacher: What do you think you are going to find in that hole, Jasmine?

(Jasmine continues to dig hole with her hands.)

(Lots of yelling in background from other children.)

Child: Come here.

Child: Look!

(Children gather.)

Teacher: Stay still, William. He's not going to hurt you. He's green. Now, where did you find this bug?

Child: On his shirt.

Teacher: Don't pull him—you're going to hurt him. See it on your shirt, William? If you look closely. We want to be very careful because it's so little, we don't want to squoosh him. We want to be very gentle. Can we get him on the pen or is he going to fly away? Does he have wings? There he is.

(Teacher gets bug onto the pen.)

Teacher: Sit down and I'll show you. Sit down over here so everybody can see. What kind of an animal do you think this is?

(Children gather around the teacher.)

Karen: Can I put him in my hand?

Teacher: Do you want to try to put him in your hands?

(Karen cups the bug in her hands.)

Teacher: Where did you find him, William?

William: He flew on my shirt.

Teacher: He flew on your shirt. Wow! I wonder where he came from.

Scene 2: In the classroom, the same children are sitting around a table with their teacher.

Teacher: Kevin, what about you? What else did you find?

Kevin: I found a spider *(inaudible)*.

Teacher: Yes, you did find a spider. Where did you find the spider? *(Teacher shows her clipboard to Kevin.)* See, I have it on my chart all the things that we found when we went outside. I wrote it down.

Kevin: I found my spider in the grass.

Teacher: What about you, Karen? What did you find at the playground? What kind of animal did you see?

Karen: I found an ant and I found more ants . . . and more.

Teacher: So you found a lot of ants. Where did you find your ants?

Karen: I found them in the grass.

Teacher: You were moving the grass around and you saw them in the grass? And where else?

Karen: Then they were going to the house. They were sleeping because they want to sleep and then they tired and the house [is] going to be dark.

Teacher: What do you think the ants eat? How can we keep them alive?

Karen: Because we don't want to keep them out of the home.

Teacher: Okay. So, we need to let them in their home to keep them alive. And what are they going to eat? What do ants eat?

Child: Grass.

Teacher: Grass, maybe.

Karen: Because ants eat sand. Because *(inaudible)* outside

Teacher: Okay, Dione, what did you find? What kind of animals did you find?

Dione: Spiders.

Teacher: Spiders. What else?

READ AND REFLECT 4:
OPEN EXPLORATION

Name: _____

Make a copy of the "Observation Record" on p. 143 of *Discovering Nature with Young Children.* Document observations of four or five children during an open exploration outdoors. Reflect on your observations and complete the questions below. Bring your observation record and your reflections to workshop 4.

1. What evidence did you see of children's interest in exploring nature? Include specific comments and behaviors of the children.

2. What connections can you make between children's engagement and the science outcomes on pp. 147–153 of the teacher's guide? Look in the naturalist behaviors column for examples similar to those of the children.

3. What will you want to accomplish on your next outdoor exploration? What might improve the quality of children's engagement? How can you extend experiences they have had? How can you draw in new children?

4. How would you rate the quality of your observation notes? Did you record descriptive details that were useful when reflecting? What might you want to do differently next time?

BASIC WORKSHOP 4

Focused Exploration of Animals

AT A GLANCE

Purpose:

- Engage in a focused exploration of an animal
- Deepen understanding of the science concepts and inquiry skills
- Experience the teacher's role as a facilitator of focused exploration

Activity	Time: 1.5 hours	Materials
Discuss Observation Ask teachers to share open exploration observations briefly.	20 minutes	• "Read and Reflect 4"
Focused Exploration of Mealworms Facilitate an indoor exploration of an animal with an emphasis on observation of the body, its parts, and the relation of those parts to its behavior. The teacher's role will be modeled by encouraging inquiry and engagement with the science concepts.	1 hour and 10 minutes	• Overhead projector, screen, and overheads 4.1 and 4.2 • Mealworms • Paper plates • Hand lenses • Charts and markers • Reference books • Camera and film (optional) • Copies of "Read and Reflect 5"

Pre-assignment: Conduct observation of an outdoor exploration and complete reflection questions.

Basic Workshop 4: Focused Exploration of Animals

Objectives

Purpose:

- Engage in a focused exploration of an animal
- Deepen understanding of the science concepts and inquiry skills
- Experience the teacher's role as a facilitator of focused exploration

Overview

- Discuss observation (20 minutes)
- Focused exploration of mealworms (1 hour and 10 minutes)

Instructor Preparation

Purchase mealworms at a nearby pet store (call ahead to be sure they have regular mealworms in stock). Be sure to have at least one mealworm per participant. You might have to purchase a container of fifty or more.

Mealworms are actually the larval stage of an insect, and therefore not really "worms." With a hand lens you can see their six legs. Mealworms are great to have in the classroom because they are easy to handle and observe, and because they undergo a four-stage life cycle, as do many other insects. As with butterflies, each stage of a mealworm's life looks very different from what preceded it, which is part of what makes mealworms so fascinating.

Mealworms begin as eggs. Out of the eggs hatch tiny larvae, and as they eat and grow they become the mealworms that are sold at pet stores. At pet stores they are refrigerated to keep them in the larval stage as long as possible so they can be used as food for a variety of reptiles and amphibians which prefer to eat the larvae. When left at room temperature, however, they will eventually continue to undergo metamorphosis into the pupa stage, which looks somewhat different from the larval "worm"—in fact, many people will think they have died. The adult, a brown or black beetle, will emerge from the pupa. The adults will mate, lay eggs, and then die. If you keep the container for several months, you are likely to begin to notice very small mealworms—a new generation!

It is difficult to predict how long this process will take, based on the temperature at which they are kept and how old they are when you purchase them, but you can count on some changes happening within three or four weeks.

You will find additional information about mealworms in the "Resources" section (p. 125) in the teacher's guide.

Review steps 3–6 in "Focused Exploration: Animals." You will be modeling an exploration with elements of these steps. This review will help you understand the elements of the exploration and strategies you might use for engaging teachers.

Materials

- Mealworms (three or four for each group of three)
- Paper plates (one for each group)
- Hand lenses

- Charts: "We Notice . . ." and "We Wonder . . ." (include a column for each of the types of questions discussed in session 1), and, for each group of three a chart labeled "What We Learned About Mealworms . . . " (make three columns: "Our Question," "What We Did," and "What We Learned")

- Reference books (use during the exploration)

- Camera and film (optional)

- Overhead projector, screen, and overheads 4.1 and 4.2

- Copies of "Read and Reflect 5"

Activity

Discuss Observation (20 minutes)

Purpose: This brief conversation will give teachers a chance to share experiences and give you some information about their engagement with the material you have presented. Hopefully, they will continue the conversation in informal settings.

Facilitate a brief conversation in which your teachers have a chance to share their early experiences with open exploration. You might ask questions like these:

- What kinds of plants and animals have children found in their early exploration?

- How are children showing their interest?

- What connections have you made to the science outcomes?

- What next steps are you planning?

If issues arise and there is no time to problem solve, be sure to let your teachers know how you will follow up with them.

Focused Exploration of Mealworms (1 hour 10 minutes)

Purpose: This experience will provide teachers with a deeper understanding of the science concepts, inquiry skills, and focused exploration—its purpose, the nature of activities, and the role that teachers play in facilitating children's inquiry.

1. **Introduce the activity** (10 minutes). Tell teachers they will be engaged in an indoor focused exploration of mealworms. Mention that you will be modeling the strategies they can use to engage their children in exploration and inquiry. As with the exploration they did in workshop 1, this exploration has been designed for adults. Much of this can be used with children. Tell participants you'll save a few minutes to discuss this later. Do the following to prepare:

   - Ask teachers to form groups of three.

   - Pass out a few mealworms to each group.

   - Ask groups to spend a few minutes just observing and thinking about questions they might have.

   - Remind them to take notes.

Show the reference books you have and tell them where you are putting them. Remember to take pictures as they explore.

2. **DISCUSS THEIR INITIAL REACTIONS** for about five minutes. After a few minutes, ask each group to share two or three observations and two or three questions from their notes. Go around the room until there are no more new ones. List these on the charts prepared for the session ("We Notice . . ." and "We Wonder . . .").

> Teachers will see things like the color and shape of the mealworms, the variation among them, and the parts of their bodies.
>
> They will wonder things like, "Why are some not moving? What do they eat? Drink? Are they like earthworms, which don't like light? Are they more active at night? Can we tell the male and female apart? Where do they live? How do they reproduce?"

Ask why they think you are starting this way, and let a few teachers share their thoughts. Make the point that inquiry is promoted when naturalists communicate what they are finding and thinking. Share that this is an important step with children too.

3. **CONTINUE THE EXPLORATION** (15 minutes). Ask your teachers to stay in their groups for the next fifteen-minute activity. Show overhead 4.1 with the instructions.

OVERHEAD 4.1: ACTIVITY INSTRUCTIONS

1. List what you already know about mealworms.

2. List questions you have about mealworms.

3. Observe and note features, behavior, and similarities and differences.

4. Draw what you see.

5. Add to your original list of questions.

Listen and watch what teachers are doing. Notice what they are saying about the mealworms and how their comments relate to what they can actually observe about the mealworms. You might want to make a few notes so you can refer to these comments and observations later when talking about inquiry questions.

4. **PROCESS AGAIN** (10 minutes). After about fifteen minutes of exploration, bring everyone together in the large group and ask for some comments.

   a. Ask teachers to share a few of their observations and questions. As they share, list the questions on the prepared chart.

   b. Talk about categorizing questions. Put up overhead 4.2 with the categories and ask them to consider them again. Guide them as they categorize their questions.

> ## OVERHEAD 4.2: QUESTION CATEGORIES
>
> 1. **Questions I can answer by observation**
>
> 2. **Questions I can answer through experiments I can set up**
>
> 3. **Questions I can answer through other sources like books, the Internet, and experts**

c. You might also ask in what ways drawing the worms was helpful in generating questions. "Did you notice new things as you drew?" Take about ten minutes for this debriefing.

5. **RESUME THE EXPLORATION** (15 minutes). Tell teachers that you would like them to select one of the questions to investigate. Remind them that they have been engaged in open exploration and are now moving into focused exploration. Tell people they will need to select a question that can be answered by observation or by simple experiment. They will have fifteen minutes to identify a question and begin to plan how they will find an answer. Remind people that this will be a short time, and they are unlikely to finish.

Ask each group to write down their questions, describe their plans, and record initial observations and ideas on a chart labeled "What We Learned About Mealworms . . ." with three columns ("Our Questions," "What We Did," and "What We Learned"). Tell them that this chart will be posted at the end of the activity so each group can look at each other's findings and ask some questions.

They will need a few minutes to establish which question they'll pursue, and then to conduct an exploration. Your goal will be to get each group focused on a particular question with ideas for how they will find the answer. Some will come up with their own questions and others will need your help. Do the following as you go to each group:

- Observe and listen. Note what children are saying and doing, the language they use, how they go about collecting new information, the level of collaboration among children. You can reflect on these things later as you make points about their inquiry.

- Offer encouragement. If groups are having difficulty, you might help them to find a question by first asking what they have noticed about the mealworms, then suggesting a question based on something they noticed. For instance, they might have noticed that the mealworms seem to move forward by using their legs. You could ask, "Do the mealworms ever move backward? If so, how do they do it?" If the group seems interested in this question, encourage them to see how they can answer it.

- Suggest questions that help teachers look more closely. For example, you might ask the following:

  – How do mealworms move? How can we find out?

  – Do mealworms prefer a particular kind of environment? Light or dark? Damp or dry?

  – How are the mealworms alike? How are they different?

  – What do they prefer to eat? How might we find out?

- Take photos (optional). Your photos could be used to model documentation panel making for advanced workshop 14.

6. **Process again** (10 minutes). After ten to fifteen minutes, remind each group to begin filling in the chart "What We Learned About Mealworms . . ." Ask that the chart be posted so each group can walk around the room to see what others have done. Encourage people to talk with other groups about their experiences.

Chart Example

Our Questions	What We Did	What We Learned
What kind of environment do mealworms like?	• Put five mealworms in the middle of a plate. • Placed the following different parts of plate: potting soil, sand, shredded newspaper, and container of water.	Found four worms under paper and one in middle. We think they like the dark.
How do they move?	• Observe for a while • Put food or obstacle out	• Use six legs, all in front • Can cling • Still wonder if they move backwards

7. **Talk about your role in the previous exploration** (5 minutes). Ask, "Was there anything I said or did during this exploration that helped or didn't help you to get involved and engage in inquiry?" Use this conversation as a way to elevate the modeling you have done and call attention to the impact of particular strategies, such as the kinds of questions you asked and the way the activities were structured.

8. **In closing, collect** "Read and Reflect 4" and distribute "Read and Reflect 5" and confirm the time and place of your next workshop.

READ AND REFLECT 5:
FOCUSED EXPLORATION

Name: _____

Before coming to workshop 5 read focused exploration and extensions in the teacher's guide. Observe a small group of children (two to four) engaged in exploring nature and complete an observation record (p. 143 in teacher's guide). Respond to these questions as you reflect on what you read and observed. This information will be helpful in the workshop discussion.

In workshop 5 we will talk about three purposes of focused exploration. What examples of these can you find in the focused exploration steps?

1. Help children gain deeper understanding of plants and animals. How exactly does focused exploration do this? What teaching strategies (refer to the teacher's role in "Resources") are key?

2. Encourages continued use of indoor and outdoor environments. When and how does focused exploration do this? How does it connect the two?

3. What challenges will you face as you implement focused exploration for the first time?

Reflect on Observation

1. What science concepts were the children exploring? Refer to the outcomes chart and make specific connections between the concepts listed and children's comments and behaviors.

2. What science inquiry skills were the children using? Refer to the science outcomes chart in the teacher's guide and make specific connections between the skills listed and children's comments and behaviors.

3. What evidence did you see of the children's readiness for focused exploration?

Overview of Focused Exploration

AT A GLANCE

Purpose:

- Become familiar with focused exploration, its purpose and its sequence
- Gain basic understanding of the teacher's role during focused exploration
- Continue to build understanding of the science concepts and inquiry skills and how they are expressed in children's behaviors and conversation
- Begin to understand what children's exploration in focused exploration might look like
- Build deeper understanding of the difference between open exploration and focused exploration, as well as the transition between the two

Activity	Time: 1.5 hours	Materials
Discuss Observation Facilitate a conversation in which teachers share their classroom experiences	30 minutes	• "Read and Reflect 5" • Overheads 1.1 and 1.2
A Closer Look at Focused Exploration Give teachers an overview of focused exploration, its purpose and flow. Connect their mealworm exploration to this content. Use a vignette to illustrate what focused exploration looks like in a classroom.	1 hour	• VCR, monitor, and video cued to vignette 3 • Copies of vignette observation form (in basic workshop 3), transcript to video vignette 3, and "Read and Reflect 6" • Overhead projector, screen, and overheads 5.1–5.3

Pre-assignment: Read focused exploration and extensions. Conduct an observation and respond to reflection questions.

Basic Workshop 5: Overview of Focused Exploration

OBJECTIVES

- Become familiar with focused exploration, its purpose and sequence

- Gain basic understanding of the teacher's role during focused exploration

- Continue to build understanding of the science concepts and inquiry skills and how they are expressed in children's behavior and conversation

- Begin to understand what children's exploration in focused exploration might look like

- Build deeper understanding of the difference between open exploration and focused exploration, as well as the transition between the two

OVERVIEW

- Discuss observations (30 minutes)

- Overview of focused exploration (1 hour)

INSTRUCTOR PREPARATION

- **PREVIEW VIDEO VIGNETTE 3.** Prepare for using the video vignette by previewing it and identifying the key points you want to make about these children and their teacher. The vignette shows the children exploring seedlings. Vignette 4 shows children engaged in observation of worms and would also be useful when discussing focused exploration. Instructions for using vignette 4 are in advanced workshop 8, p. 95.

MATERIALS

- Video vignette 3, VCR, and monitor

- Overhead projector, screen, overheads 1.2, 1.3, 5.1, 5.2, and 5.3

- Copies of the vignette observation form (in basic workshop 3), transcript to video vignette 3

Activity

DISCUSS OBSERVATIONS (30 MINUTES)

PURPOSE: Provide another opportunity for sharing experiences, addressing issues that have surfaced, and encouraging collaboration between teachers.

Facilitate sharing classroom experiences using these questions to guide the conversation: (You might show overhead 1.2: Inquiry diagram and 1.3: Science Concepts during this conversation.)

- What inquiry skills have children been using? Probe for specific evidence to support their statements.

- What science concepts are your children exploring? Again, probe for specifics.

- How do you plan to encourage further inquiry and promote deeper science understandings? Spend some time helping them think about this, using the teacher guide as a reference.

You might want to collect and review teacher's observation and reflection. You will get a sense of how well they understand the workshop content. You will also get ideas for follow-up.

A CLOSE LOOK AT FOCUSED EXPLORATION (45 MINUTES)

PURPOSE: This interactive activity will familiarize teachers with focused exploration, its purpose and its flow. They will gain a deeper understanding of young children's inquiry and what it looks like in the classroom. Help teachers make connections to their focused exploration of mealworms that will deepen their understanding.

1. **PROVIDE OVERVIEW OF FOCUSED EXPLORATION** using three overheads. (Take no more than 30 minutes for this.) Refer teachers to the focused observation section of the teacher's guide. Tell them that you are going to help them understand the purpose and flow of activity in their role as a teacher, and how children might be engaged.

   a. Introduce focused exploration by reviewing overhead 5.1.

OVERHEAD 5.1: PURPOSE OF FOCUSED EXPLORATION

- **Give children opportunities to investigate specific questions in depth**
  The term "focused" refers to the investigation of a particular question or idea about living things over time and from multiple perspectives. The term "investigation" implies that the children are deepening their use of inquiry through prediction, planning, data collection, and analysis. Children's understandings grow as they pursue their own particular interests and questions.

- **Give children the support, materials, and time they need to deepen their exploration**
  Whether in open or focused exploration, time, materials, and support are always key to inquiry based science. Continue both indoor and outdoor exploration, and remember that the teacher's role as a guide is key when it is time to engage in the more advanced skills of inquiry like data collection and analysis.

In reference to the last bullet, refer to the assignment and ask for examples of inquiry skills used in focused exploration. You might want to put up the inquiry diagram and refer to parts of it, and ask for examples from their reading. Do this quickly, taking just a few examples.

Ask about the role of the extensions, making the point that they provide the children with important information about naturalists and their work. In the process, they gain insight into how they can be naturalists themselves and the kinds of people, books, and experiences that are important sources of information. In addition, these activities also lead to the answers of important questions.

Help teachers to make connections to their experiences in the last exploration by asking, "What specific activities did you engage in during the animal exploration that would exemplify focused exploration?" Question further by asking, "How was that different from being engaged in open exploration?"

This conversation will focus on deeper exploration of an idea or organism and the use of inquiry skills. Be sure these ideas are discussed:

• Selected a question and planned an investigation

• Recorded observations and represented experiences

• Reflected on experience, found patterns across groups, and constructed explanations as we compiled what we know

• Asked new questions

• Explored science content and how inquiry deepened understanding of content

Show overhead 5.2 and review the elements of focused exploration for animals and plants. Refer the teachers to p. 20 in the "Getting Ready" section of the teacher's guide during this conversation.

Overhead 5.2: Elements of Focused Exploration

• **The tree or bush study**
Over the course of the year the children observe the changes in a tree on a monthly basis. They document their study in a book.

• **Ongoing explorations indoors and outdoors**
Two or three times a week, the children's exploration is focused on particular plants outdoors and in their terrarium.

• **Focus on plants**
Children start a variety of indoor plants at the beginning of the school year and observe their growth and change over the course of the year.

• **Focus on animals**
Beginning with an outdoor search for small animals that become short-term visitors in the classroom, the focus encourages investigation of animals' characteristics, needs, and habitats.

---

b. Help teachers think about how these elements might play out over a year. Talk about the sample calendars in the right-hand column. Make these points:

• Plan for this exploration to take place during several periods over the school year.

• The cycle will always be repeated: engage, explore, reflect.

• Within each of these elements a sequence of activities is carefully constructed.

• The monthly tree observation, weekly outdoor exploration, and indoor work are done simultaneously while focused on plants.

• In both the plant and animal sections, teachers are given examples of ways they can help children pursue their interests or questions about particular physical characteristics or one of their behaviors.

c. Use overhead 5.3 to discuss the transition from open to focused exploration. (Refer them to p. 38 in the teacher's guide.) Connect these points back to comments they made when discussing their observations. Help them understand who in their class-rooms is showing signs of being ready to focus.

OVERHEAD 5.3: THE TRANSITION FROM OPEN EXPLORATION TO FOCUSED EXPLORATION

Children who are ready to move into focused exploration will show signs like these:

- **Show interest in observing a particular plant or animal from one day to the next**
  You may see children returning to an outdoor site or the terrarium repeatedly. They may connect their observations from one day to another or begin to ask questions about what they are observing.

- **Wonder about a particular aspect or characteristic of a living thing**
  Children may show interest in how an animal moves or eats, how quickly a plant grows, or what it looks like underground.

- **Do research in books to find photos or information about plants or animals they observed**
  They may want to identify a plant or animal, learn its name, or find out some fact such as how many legs it has or what it eats.

Connect these ideas to those on overhead 5.1 by sharing that these children are engaged in inquiry by exploring important ideas about the characteristics, behaviors, growth and development, and needs of living things. Point out that focused exploration will help children look more closely at living things, and think about ideas such as how the functions of plants' different parts help them grow. It will also help children move from broad observations to more complex exploration of plants and animals.

2. **VIEW AND DISCUSS VIGNETTE 3** (30 minutes). Introduce the vignette by saying that it was taped in a Head Start classroom in Boston. The children are a mixed-age group; they speak approximately nine languages among them. This vignette shows five English language learners examining their seedlings. (Below you will find suggestions for talking about this aspect of the vignette with teachers.) Explain to teachers that they will view the vignette twice.

   a. Before the first viewing, distribute the transcript. Tell teachers to note the children's engagement and learning as they watch the vignette. Show the vignette and then let them share their comments for a few minutes.

   b. Prepare them for the second viewing of the video by giving each teacher a copy of the vignette observation form. Ask them to focus on the children's engagement and the strategies the teacher uses to focus their observations of the seedlings.

   c. Show the video and give them a few minutes to record observations and thoughts.

   d. Bring groups together and guide a discussion using the following questions:

   - Why would you characterize this vignette as a focused exploration? Probe for specific examples.

   - This teacher played a key role in the children's experience. What did she do to encourage engagement and guide inquiry?

You may want to highlight the following points when discussing vignette 3.

Look for ideas like these about the children's engagement and focused exploration:

- The children are investigating a particular plant over time—they have planted seedlings and are watching them grow. As they observe they identify the parts of the plant and watch how they change over time.

- They are engaged in inquiry as they observe closely (use magnifying glasses and look for parts of plant), record what they see (draw representations in their journals and learn to label), compare it to the poster, and consider questions (when wondering where the seed is they are considering how the plant has changed). They are constructing reasonable responses.

- While these children are not particularly articulate about what they see, their interest and what they understand is definitely indicated. For example, they make references to the parts of plants, sometimes using names of parts. They may recognize the similarity between their seedlings and the ones in the poster, or have reasonable theories about where the seed went. Even something as subtle as picking the green marker to draw a plant when given a choice of colors is a sign of understanding about the nature of plants and a desire to represent them accurately.

Look for these ideas about the role the teacher plays:

- Values what children are doing by spending time with them and repeating their ideas.

- Teaches the children to take care of plants, reminding them to be careful and allowing them to spray water on plants while they work.

- Creates an environment and provides tools—poster, seedlings and spray bottles, journals, hand lenses, and markers.

- Uses questions that focus the children's observation—What parts do you see? Where did the seed go?

- Uses vocabulary the children are learning and translates into written words—*seed, stem, leaves, grow,* and *plant.*

- Helps children articulate their ideas—"When you look in the magnifying glass, the plant appears much bigger."

- Helps Ronnie get the right color for his drawing.

Strategies being used to support the engagement of the second language learners:

Note that these strategies are effective with all children, but are particularly effective with second language learners. Their extended engagement is testimony to the teacher's abilities. She employs the following practices:

- Uses simple sentences

- Provides a chart or illustration to which the children can relate

- Repeats what children have said, corrects their grammar and vocabulary errors

- Uses many important terms in a context that gives words meaning—the descriptive terms for the different shades of greens, the concept of tiny, the parts of the plants

- Listens carefully and interprets the children's meaning

- Helps Daphne label her picture in a way that reflects her ideas

- Is enthusiastic

- Encourages literacy development by reading the chart

The teacher is also sensitive to concepts that might be hard for children to understand. While she uses the term "wondering," which they might not understand, she follows up with precise language that communicates her real meaning.

e. In conclusion, refer teachers again to "The Teacher's Roles," p.115 in "Resources" in their teacher's guide. They will find further description of strategies to use during focused exploration here. Collect "Read and Reflect 5" and distribute "Read and Reflect 6." Remind teachers of the time and place for the next workshop.

TRANSCRIPT OF VIDEO VIGNETTE 3:
FOCUSED EXPLORATION OF BEAN SEEDLINGS

Scene 1: Five children—Victor *(in sweatshirt)*, Armin *(in white T-shirt)*, Thalia *(in red and white striped shirt)*, Roney *(in plaid shirt)*, and Daphne *(in denim overalls)*—are sitting around a table examining their seedlings with their teacher, Cindy.

The children are looking at their seedlings and interacting with each other as the teacher enters.

Teacher: *(Inaudible)* when you are pulling it out, I want you to be very careful. Look at it and tell me what you see.

Armin: This one is growing up. *(Examines plant in cup.)*

Teacher: It's growing up and what parts do you see? What parts do you see? *(Pointing to Victor's seedling.)*

Victor: *(Inaudible)*

Teacher: Be very careful, Victor. You don't want it to break.

Teacher: *(To Thalia)* What do you see? What parts of the plant do you see? Do you see any stem going up?

Armin: I see a flower on it.

Teacher: You see a flower on it. Do you see any leaves?

Victor: Leaves, yea!

Teacher: What do you see Roney? Do you see any little leaves on yours? Roney has little tiny leaves.

Child: No, he took it off.

Teacher: Victor, you want to be very careful with your plant. Armin, if you are breaking it I am afraid it won't grow. Oh, oh, wow, let's see. What do you think we should do now?

Armin: Take it off.

Teacher: Take it off? What we are going to do—I am going to give you each a piece of paper and we are going to very carefully take your plant out and lay it on the paper so you can look at it more closely. Okay? Very carefully. You can take the whole towel out. I wouldn't pull it by the stem.

(Victor pulls out the plant and looks at the root, wrapped in wet paper towel.)

Teacher: Wow! What is under there? *(Teacher holds up Victor's plant to examine the bottom.)* Put it down on the paper so you can get a better look, and I am going to get the magnifying glass. What is that part growing down? One part grew up and one part grew down.

Victor: Yea, what is that? I got that. *(Victor examines Daphne's stem.)*

Teacher: Do you want to help Roney?

Armin: Take this out. *(He reaches toward Roney.)*

Teacher: Wow! You have a bunch growing in there. *(Teacher puts it on paper.)*

Armin: Roney, *(Inaudible)* this, oh, his broke.

Teacher: I wonder if we . . . very gently, Roney, very gently peel it off there. *(Helps Armin place a magnifier over plant.)* This kind is neat because you can put it right over. But, I want you to be careful when you put it over, that the stem doesn't break.

Daphne: Oh, it's too big.

Teacher: It is too big. Tell me what you see when you look at the bottom part.

(Daphne puts the glass carefully on the plant and examines it.)

Teacher: Tell me what you see when you look at the bottom part.

(Teacher talks to Thalia about washing the magnifying glasses.)

Child: This one is growing like a crab.

Teacher: It's growing like a crab.

(All the children are using magnifying glasses now.)

Teacher: Do you want to take that one out? *(Helps child with another plastic cup.)*

Victor: *(Inaudible)* it's bigger.

Teacher: When you look in the glass, it is much bigger. Do you know what I'm wondering? Did this thing come from the seed? Right. It grew from the seed. Where did the seed go?

Victor: *(Shrugs)* I know where.

Teacher: Where did the seed go, Armin, after your seed started to grow? Where did the brown part go?

Armin: *(Points to something on paper)* Right here.

Teacher: Do you think that is it there? Do you think it kind of fell off? Daphne, what do you think? Do you have a brown part on the bottom of your plant? *(Addresses Armin)* Do you think we can gently move the towel away so we can see the plant better? Very gently so that you don't break the roots.

Armin: I can. *(Teacher pulls off towel.)*

Armin: Towels are wet.

Teacher: They're very wet. Why did we wet them? Do you remember—why did we spray them with water?

Victor: *(Looking through magnifying glass)* Mine looks bigger now.

Teacher: Looks bigger. You can keep pulling that towel off. Daphne, try pulling off your towel. Thalia is washing the magnifying glass. She will be right back. Very gently. *(Teacher helps her.)* What did you find?

Child: I'm going to wash this one. Can I wash this one?

Teacher: You know what? I think the other ones were clean. I'm just going to have Thalia wash one. We can wash them when we are done maybe. Okay, after everyone can spray theirs.

(Victor is using spray bottle on plant lying on paper.)

Teacher: *(To Victor)* I want you to take a look at yours. Take a look at that root. Is that the seed? Is that where it is all started? Thalia's seed is still there. Look, Armin. Is that her seed? She thinks it is.

Teacher: Daphne, what about yours? Did you see your seed at the bottom, or did your seed fall off? *(Lifts Daphne's seedling and replaces it on the paper. Daphne points to the leaves.)* What do you think? Do you think that might be the seed? How do you think it got up there?

Daphne: Yah. It was moving.

Teacher: It was moving? Do you think it moved when it was growing? It moved up to the top?

(Daphne sprays plant.)

Victor: *(Looking through magnifying glass)* Cindy, want to see? It looks bigger.

Teacher: It looks much bigger. How big does it look?

Victor: A lot bigger.

Teacher: Actually, oh, it's not coming out? I see water on Daphne's paper.

Victor: Water?

Teacher: Okay, Armin, one thing we don't want to do . . . we don't want to get water on your science journals because that will make the marker part very messy. Okay? *(Teacher hands out journals—children start drawing in their journals.)*

Armin: Maybe we take that off.

Teacher: What if we move it? What if we move it? Because I want you to be able to look at your plant while you are drawing. What if I just move it up a little bit here? *(She moves his paper with seedling up on the table and puts his journal in from of him.)*

Victor: *(Off camera)* What color do you want? Black?

Teacher: Okay, Roney, your [plant] is . . . Roney's is very small. Do you want to use yours or do you want to find a bigger one? Do you want to use this one or do you want to look for a bigger one?

Roney: This one.

Teacher: That one. Okay.

(Thalia hands Roney a red marker.)

Teacher: You know what? Look at the color of Roney's plant. What color do you think he needs?

Thalia: I gave it to Roney.

Teacher: I know you gave it to Roney, and you are helping Roney and that makes me happy. But I'm wondering why you gave Roney a red marker?

Thalia: I got a green one.

Teacher: You got a pale green. I see some different shades of green *(pointing to paper)*. I see some very, very, very light green in the stem and I see some darker green.

Victor: Cindy, look at Cindy. *(He holds out hands.)*

Teacher: I see some light green in yours and I see some dark green underneath. Armin, I want you to take a good look at the plant before you start drawing. And remember there's different colors of green in here *(lifting markers)*, and there is also brown and black. And if you need any other colors, we can get some in our other marker basket. Roney, did you need any other color?

(Roney picks green marker and says something inaudible.)

Daphne: *(Pointing to something)* What *(inaudible)* is that?

Teacher: What do you see over here? *(Points to doc panel on wall.)* Do you see a seed over here like the ones that you planted? And then what happened to the seed over here?

Daphne: It got planted.

Teacher: It got planted and what's happening here? Can I read what it says under the picture? It says, "A bean seed is planted in the ground." Number two, "A root grows from the seed." Number three, "A stem pushes up through the ground." Number four says, "Leaves grow on the stem."

(Teacher then sits at the table next to Daphne.)

Teacher: Is [it] okay if I write down the parts that you told me so we don't forget? Show me where this part that looks like a seed shape [goes]. *(Daphne points to something in her journal)* Can I write it? Do you want me to write it, or do you want to write it?

Daphne: You.

Teacher: What should I say? That it's the part that looks like a seed? *(Daphne shakes her head yes and teacher writes in her journal.)* Now show me the stem part. I wrote, "Part looks like seed." Show me the stem part. Was it this one? *(Daphne points and the teacher writes "stem.")* That one, okay. Stem. Then what abut the roots? Show me where the roots are in your picture. Right over there? Okay. Oh, I see another long part. Look it. Another stem part. Roots. All right. *(Daphne points)* Would you like me to write "stem" and "roots" and "seed" on paper? In fact, I think we have it. Would you like me to write those words on paper for you? We should have it.

READ AND REFLECT 6:
FOCUSED EXPLORATION

Name: _____

Observe a small group of children (two to four) engaged in focused exploration, and complete an observation record (p. 143 in the teacher's guide). Respond to these questions as you reflect on what you observed.

1. What characterized this activity as focused exploration?

2. What science inquiry skills were the children using? Refer to the science outcomes chart in the teacher's guide and make specific connections between the skills listed and children's comments and behaviors.

3. What science concepts were the children exploring? Refer to the outcomes chart and make specific connections between the concepts listed and your children's comments and behaviors.

4. What might be appropriate next steps for these children? Please explain how each idea will encourage further inquiry and promote deeper science understandings. Refer to specific steps in the teacher's guide.

5. How would you rate the quality of your observation notes? Did you record descriptive details that were useful when reflecting? What might you want to do differently next time?

Focused Exploration of Plants

At a Glance

Purpose:

- Engage in a focused exploration of plants
- Deepen understanding of the science concepts and inquiry skills
- Extend understanding of the teacher's role as a facilitator of focused exploration

Activity	Time: 1.5 hours	Materials
Discuss Observation Facilitate a brief exchange of teachers' observations from focused exploration.	20 minutes	• "Read and Reflect 6"
Focused Exploration of Plants Using plants that were planted in workshop 2, facilitate a focused exploration. Engage teachers in observational drawing and talk about what they notice.	1 hour and 10 minutes	• Plants planted in workshop 2 • Copies of handouts: "Plant Parts: Stems, Leaves, Roots" and "Basic Workshop Evaluation"

Pre-assignment: Complete "Read and Reflect 6," conducting an observation and responding to the reflection questions.

Workshop 6: Focused Exploration of Plants

OBJECTIVES

PURPOSE:

- Engage in a focused exploration of plants
- Deepen understanding of the science concepts and inquiry skills
- Extend understanding of the teacher's role as a facilitator

OVERVIEW

- Discuss observations (20 minutes)
- A focused exploration of plants (1 hour and 10 minutes)

INSTRUCTOR PREPARATION

- **REVIEW THE PLANTS SECTION OF FOCUSED EXPLORATION TO PREPARE.** With the steps from the teacher's guide fresh in your mind, you can make valuable connections to what participants will be doing with children.

MATERIALS

- "Read and Reflect 6"
- Plants that were planted in workshop 2
- Copies of handouts: "Plant Parts: Stems, Leaves, Roots" and "Basic Workshop Evaluation"

Activity

DISCUSS OBSERVATIONS

PURPOSE: As teachers share their experiences, you will have a chance to encourage collaboration and ongoing dialogue about science teaching. You will also be able to identify issues that need addressing.

Facilitate a conversation in which teachers share their recent experiences with focused exploration. You might use questions like these:

- What inquiry skills have you seen children using? Ask for specific evidence to support their statements.
- What science concepts are children in your classroom exploring? Again, ask for specifics.
- How do you plan to encourage further inquiry and promote deeper science understandings? Spend some time helping them think about this. Use the teacher guide as a reference.

> You might want to collect and review their observation and reflection. You will get a sense of how well they are understanding the workshop content and get ideas for follow-up.

Be sure to let teachers know how you will follow up on issues that don't get resolved in this conversation.

A FOCUSED EXPLORATION OF PLANTS (1 HOUR 10 MINUTES)

PURPOSE: This activity will familiarize teachers with the experiences children will have as they engage in focused exploration of plants and the role that teachers play in facilitating children's inquiry.

> While this is the only activity designed to look at the plants teachers started in workshop 2, ideally you will continue to care for and observe these plants when the workshop is over.

1. **INTRODUCE THE ACTIVITY** (5 minutes) by telling your teachers they will be using the plants they began in workshop 2 to engage in a focused exploration of plants. Use these steps to prepare:

   - Ask teachers to form groups of three or four.

   - Pass out a variety of plants begun in workshop 2 to each group. Each group should have at least one bulb, one set of germinating bean seeds, and one beet or carrot top. Each group should also have at least one houseplant. If more plants are available, distribute them evenly among the groups.

   - Ask everyone to spend a few minutes observing the various plants, thinking and talking about questions they might have.

   - Ask each group to assign someone to take notes about group members' plant observations. Tell them to jot down what they notice or observe, as well as their questions.

2. **PROCESS THEIR INITIAL REACTIONS** (10 minutes). Bring everyone together in a large group. Ask each smaller group to share two or three observations they have made about the plants. List these on the chart you have prepared for the session ("We Notice . . ." and "We Wonder . . .").

> Teachers are likely to remember how the seeds looked when they were planted and notice changes, such as seed swelling, shoots or roots, or new leaves.
> They are likely to wonder about how new leaves can grow from carrot tops, why some of these plants don't need more light, or how plants can grow without soil.

3. **CONTINUE THE EXPLORATION** (20 minutes), focusing on plant parts. Ask teachers to stay in their groups for the next thirty-minute activity. Distribute handout: "Plant Parts: Stems, Leaves, Roots." Each person should, with each of at least two plants, look very carefully at the stems, leaves, and roots. Ask teachers to use a hand lens to help them make these observations:

   - Draw the part

   - Describe the part in words

   - Jot down thoughts about what this part does for the plant

   As teachers explore the plant parts, walk around the room to offer assistance. When possible, try to connect what people are observing to their experiences with outdoor plants. You might ask, "Did plants outside have any parts that resembled this one? What do you remember about some of the stems from outdoor plants?" Also encourage teachers to compare the parts found on a single plant: "Are all the leaves on this plant the same size or shape?" These questions will help teachers focus on plant diversity and variation.

4. **PROCESS AGAIN** (10 minutes) in a large group. Ask teachers to share some of their observations:

   - What were some of the words teachers used to make verbal descriptions?

   - In what ways did drawing the plant parts help them?

   - What did they think the various plant parts might be for?

   These questions will help teachers begin to focus on the diversity of plants and the relationship between a plant part and the whole plant. Remind teachers that this experience was designed for them as adult learners, to raise some of the same ideas that they would want children to address, but in a different way. We want children to begin to draw what they observe, describe it, and wonder about it, but their abilities and experiences are different from ours.

5. **CONTINUE THE EXPLORATION** (20 minutes) by encouraging them to consider two things:

   a. How can they keep track of each plant's growth and development over time? Ask groups to make plans to follow these plants over time. Tell them to talk together about the qualities that will determine the plants' growth and development and to write down their ideas.

   b. What experiments might they try that will answer questions about plants, such as whether plants can grow in the dark, how long plants can grow without soil, whether plants would grow with some liquid other than water, and so on?
   Walk around the room to talk with people about some of their ideas. If no one seems to be coming up with the concept of measurement, be sure to suggest it. Measurement can include plant height, girth or thickness, length of roots, or size of leaves. See step 2 of "Focused Exploration: Plants" in the teacher's guide, p. 46, for suggestions for measuring and keeping track of plants. (Ideally you will actually be able to follow this process, for at least two weeks, and will really be able to see some change.)

6. BRIEFLY HAVE PEOPLE SHARE EXPERIMENTS THEY'D LIKE TO TRY (5 minutes), and, if feasible, how they can follow up with what others are observing and learning.

To conclude, distribute the basic workshop evaluation and have your teachers complete it, if time allows, or arrange to collect it later. Let the teachers know how you will be following up and supporting their implementation of the teacher's guide.

Suggested Next Steps

- This is an ideal time to start a mentoring program. Teachers will be enthusiastic about using the teacher's guide, but will also have some clear ideas about the challenges.

- You might also want to start the advanced workshops soon. Give teachers a month or so to work with the curriculum. Then use the first advanced workshop to identify their interests and questions. Plan additional workshops based on their expressed needs.

- You might also want to intersperse the workshops with guided discussions. Use the guidance on p. 177 as you plan. Guided discussions provide an opportunity for teachers to share their successes and challenges as they try new approaches to teaching science.

PLANT PARTS: STEMS, LEAVES, ROOTS

Complete this form as you examine your plant.

	Draw this part	Describe it	What do you think it does for the plant?
Stem			
Leaf			
Roots			

BASIC WORKSHOP EVALUATION

Name (optional): _____

1. To what degree have the workshops helped you learn about:

    Life science

    ☐————————☐————————☐————————☐————————☐
    not at all　　　　　　*adequate*　　　　　*significant*

    Inquiry

    ☐————————☐————————☐————————☐————————☐
    not at all　　　　　　*adequate*　　　　　*significant*

    Science teaching

    ☐————————☐————————☐————————☐————————☐
    not at all　　　　　　*adequate*　　　　　*significant*

    Using the teacher's guide

    ☐————————☐————————☐————————☐————————☐
    not at all　　　　　　*adequate*　　　　　*significant*

2. Overall, I found the level of challenge to be:

    ☐————————☐————————☐————————☐————————☐
    not at all　　　　*appropriately*　　　*much too*
    challenging　　　*challenging*　　　*challenging*

    Please explain:

3. Overall, I found the workshops to be valuable to my science teaching:

    ☐————————☐————————☐————————☐————————☐
    not at all　　　　　　*valuable*　　　　*extremely*
    valuable　　　　　　　　　　　　　　　*valuable*

    Please explain:

BASIC WORKSHOP EVALUATION (CONT'D)

4. To what extent have you already applied learning from the workshops to your work?

    no application — *some application* — *extensive application*

    Please describe one approach that has had the greatest effect on children's learning:

5. What new insights have you gained about teaching an inquiry-based science curriculum? Please explain your answer (be specific):

6. What new insights have you gained about *your role* in relation to young children's science learning?

7. What questions do you still have about using the teacher's guide?

DISCOVERING NATURE WITH YOUNG CHILDREN GUIDING PRINCIPLES

- Three- to five-year-olds can experience rich, in-depth, scientific inquiry.

- Science content draws from children's experiences, is interesting and engaging, and can be explored directly and deeply over time.

- Expectations are developmentally appropriate.

- Discussion, expression, and representation are critical ways in which children reflect on and develop theories from their active work.

- Children learn from one another.

- Teachers take on specific roles that actively support and guide children's science learning.

INQUIRY

Engage, notice, wonder, question

Focus observations, clarify questions

Plan, predict, take action

Ask new questions

Explore, investigate

Observe closely

Reflect on experience, explore patterns and relationships, construct reasonable explanations

Collect, record, represent experiences and data

Share, discuss, and reflect with group; draw conclusions; formulate ideas and theories

Science Concepts

- Characteristics of living things

- Living and nonliving

- Needs of living things

- Life cycle

- Diversity and variation

- Habitat

How does this environment encourage exploration of nature?

How does this environment encourage exploration of nature?

How does this environment encourage exploration of nature?

How does this environment encourage exploration of nature?

Purpose of Open Exploration

- Give children opportunities to wonder about, notice, and explore

- Give children the support, materials, and time they need to begin their exploration

FLOW OF OPEN EXPLORATION

- Step 1: Introduce children to *Discovering Nature with Young Children*

- Step 2: Introduce children to observing living things in an indoor terrarium

- Step 3: Teach children how to use hand lenses, penlights, and trowels

- Step 4: Explore and reflect (ongoing)

ACTIVITY INSTRUCTIONS

1. List what you already know about mealworms

2. List questions you have about mealworms

3. Observe and note features, behavior, similarities, and differences

4. Draw what you see in your notebook

5. Add questions to your original list

Questions Categories

1. Questions I can answer by observation

2. Questions I can answer through experiments

3. Questions I can answer through other sources such as books, the Internet, or experts

Purpose of Focused Exploration

- To give children opportunities to investigate specific questions in more depth

- To give children the support, materials, and time they need to deepen their exploration

Elements of Focused Exploration

- The tree or bush study

- Ongoing exploration indoors and outdoors

- Focus on plants

- Focus on animals

The Transition from Open Exploration to Focused Exploration

Look for children doing the following:

- Showing interest in observing a particular plant or animal from one day to the next

- Wondering about a particular aspect or characteristic of a living thing

- Going to books to find photos or information about plants or animals they observed

advanced workshops

Overview

The eight advanced workshops are designed to build teachers' ability to engage children in scientific inquiry. Although the workshops are numbered, they are in no particular order. However, you may want to start with workshop 7: "Creating a Culture of Inquiry About Nature." In this workshop, teachers assess their skills as science teachers. The results can help you create a sequence of workshops that responds to the interests and needs of teachers. All of the ninety-minute workshops use an instructional approach that encourages application of new ideas. The presentation of new material is combined with activities that encourage teachers to apply what they are learning as they analyze classroom practice and children's work, and as they plan the next steps.

The advanced workshops include the following:

7. CREATING A CULTURE OF INQUIRY ABOUT NATURE: This workshop addresses the environment and climate of a naturalist classroom, including strategies for conveying the excitement and wonder of observing and learning about living things. Teachers complete an evaluation of their skills as science teachers and develop individual goals for professional development.

8. DEEPENING CHILDREN'S SCIENCE UNDERSTANDINGS: In this workshop, teachers focus on the ways they can deepen children's science understandings by encouraging and guiding their inquiry.

9. USING BOOKS TO EXTEND SCIENCE LEARNING: This workshop helps teachers integrate books into their ongoing science exploration. The role, selection, and use of fiction and nonfiction books in naturalist work with children will be covered.

10. ASSESSING CHILDREN'S SCIENCE LEARNING: In this workshop, teachers discuss young children's science learning—the outcomes they might expect, how to document engagement and learning, and how they can use their documentation to plan next steps.

11. **Encouraging Representation:** This workshop addresses the importance of recording and representation. Strategies for encouraging children to use varied media to communicate their observations and understandings will be discussed.

12. **Using Children's Representations as Teaching Tools:** This workshop builds on workshop 5, "Encouraging Representation," by helping teachers use children's work to deepen their science understanding.

13. **Facilitating Science Talks:** This workshop provides teachers with strategies for facilitating successful large and small group science talks, often considered the most difficult aspect of science teaching.

14. **Making and Using Documentation Panels:** This workshop takes teachers through the process of making panels and addresses how these panels can be used as a springboard for stimulating discussions, reenactments, and further exploration.

ASSIGNMENTS

Each advanced workshop has a pre-assignment. Pre-assignments include readings in the teacher's guide; reflection questions; and material gathering, such as children's work, to discuss in the workshop. These assignments prepare teachers for participating fully in workshop discussions and activities. Be sure to distribute them at least one week before the workshop, emphasizing their importance.

ADVANCED WORKSHOP INSTRUCTIONS

The instructions for each workshop follow the same format as the basic workshops. Each workshop includes the following sections:

- At a Glance outlines the purpose, activities, timeline, materials, and pre-assignment for each session

- Objectives identify what skills you want teachers to gain by the end of the session

- An overview describes the activities and how much time to devote to each one

- Instructor Preparation lists the materials you need and how to prepare for each session

- Detailed step-by-step instructions provide guidance for leading each activity

- Handouts to copy for each participant

- Overheads to copy as transparencies before each session

- "Read and Reflect" pre-assignments to copy and distribute at least a week before each session for workshops 8 and 13.

Handouts, overheads, or assignments appear after most workshop's instructions. You will also find suggested next steps, which offer ideas that help teachers with follow-up, as they apply their new learnings to their classrooms.

"Next Steps" include the following:

- Strategy handouts: In many workshops, teachers develop lists of strategies they have found useful, read about in the teacher's guide, or seen in vignettes. Type up strategies and distribute them.

- Plan another workshop: Choose one that builds on the skills teachers are developing. Be sure that teachers have time to work with the content of at least one workshop before offering another. We suggest one-month intervals.

- Plan guided conversations: Focused conversation in small groups is an excellent way for teachers to deepen their understandings and build their ability, once the content has been presented. Help teachers create relevant documents from their classrooms to use as material that stimulates thought and discussion. For example, videotaped or audiotaped science talks would make excellent documents for discussion after workshop 13. Transcribing is also a great idea.

- Mentoring: Individual support may be the best way to support teachers. Careful examination of teachers' work supports reflective practice, while giving you the insights needed to tailor your approach based on teachers' interests and needs.

- Recommended reading: The bibliography is full of valuable books and articles. Distribute these to teachers at strategic points during the workshop. Be sure to use this material to build your understanding of science teaching and learning as well.

Creating a Culture of Inquiry About Nature

AT A GLANCE

Purpose:

- Build strategies for creating a culture of inquiry
- Assess knowledge and skills as science teachers
- Set goals for professional development as science teachers

Activity	Time	Materials
Define term "culture of inquiry" Present characteristics of a culture of inquiry and use a video vignette to illustrate your points.	40 minutes	• Chart: "Strategies for Creating a Culture of Inquiry" • VCR, monitor, and video cued to vignette 1 • Overhead projector, screen, and overhead 7.1
Complete self-assessment Engage teachers in completing the "Evaluating Science Teaching" form (p. 205). Facilitate small group discussion of needs and goals.	35 minutes	• Copies of "Evaluating Science Teaching"
Conduct collective goal setting Have groups share their goals and issues, and make plans for supporting further professional development.	15 minutes	• Copies of small group recording form • Charts: "Our Strengths as Science Teachers" and "Our Needs as Science Teachers"

Pre-assignment: Read the introduction to the teacher's guide.

Advanced Workshop 7:
Creating a Culture of Inquiry About Nature

OBJECTIVES

- Build strategies for creating a culture of inquiry about nature

- Assess knowledge and skills as science teachers

- Set goals for your own classroom

OVERVIEW

- Define term "culture of inquiry" (40 minutes)

- Complete self-assessment (35 minutes)

- Conduct collective goal setting (15 minutes)

INSTRUCTOR PREPARATION

- **ASSIGN READING.** At least one week before the workshop, ask teachers to read the introduction to *Discovering Nature with Young Children* teacher's guide.

- **CONSIDER OBSERVING TEACHERS IN THE CLASSROOM AT THIS TIME.** This will give you valuable information about teachers' science teaching. Start by deciding which parts of the "Evaluating Science Teaching" form you want to use. If your teachers are beginners, it might not be appropriate for them to use the whole form. As teachers become more skilled you will want to expand the aspects of their practice that you are focusing on. Use the following when planning your observations:

  – When evaluating beginning teachers, focus on section I A, B, and C; section II A1, A2, and B1.

  – When evaluating developing teachers, focus on the sections that you used for the beginning teacher and add section I D and the rest of section II.

  – When evaluating teachers who are refining their skills, use the whole form.

- **PREVIEW VIGNETTE 1.** Look at the vignette, being sure that you understand the points that should be made.

MATERIALS

- 3 charts: "Strategies for Creating a Culture of Inquiry," "Our Strengths as Science Teachers," and "Our Needs as Science Teachers"

- VCR, monitor, and video cued to vignette 1

- Overhead projector, screen, and overhead 7.1

- Copies of evaluating science teaching (p. 205 in planning chapter) and small group recording forms (one for each group)

Activity

DEFINE TERM "CULTURE OF INQUIRY" (40 MINUTES)

PURPOSE: To build a common understanding of the elements that contribute to a positive and productive climate for science learning.

1. **INTRODUCE THE WORKSHOP AND THE TERM "CULTURE OF INQUIRY"**
   (10 minutes). Give a quick overview of the workshop. Explain that one of the most important roles inquiry-based science teachers will play is to create a "culture of inquiry about nature." This culture promotes children's investigation of plants and animals in their natural environments with methods used by naturalists and scientists. In this environment, the physical space and the interactions convey the excitement and wonder of observing and learning about living things. Review 7.1, providing a quick overview of the elements of this culture. You will discuss them more in-depth after viewing the vignette.

OVERHEAD 7.1: THE CULTURE OF INQUIRY ABOUT NATURE

- **A respect for living things**
  A naturalist environment conveys an attitude of serious respect for living things and their habitats. It emphasizes learning about plants and animals in their natural environments and indoor mini-environments.

- **An emphasis on inquiry**
  Naturalists ask questions, observe closely over time, and think about what their observations tell them. The teacher's role is not to provide the answers, but to encourage the children to ask questions and support them as they seek answers. There is an emphasis on gathering data (or evidence) and recording it for reflection and analysis. The room is filled with children's work, photographs, charts, and panels that communicate the value of documentation.

- **Sharing observations and ideas**
  In a culture of inquiry, children are encouraged to share their observations and ideas through small and large group science talks, and they learn to listen to what others have to say.

- **Recording observations and experiences**
  Naturalists spend a great deal of time recording what they see—using careful sketches, descriptive words, and names to most accurately remember their experiences. They use their records to reflect with others and find patterns in their observations. Young naturalists, with guidance, can begin to develop these skills. Materials for representation and recording are easily accessible. Teachers support children as they document their words and ideas, and their work is used for reflecting on observations and ideas.

- **A focus on actual living things**
  The culture of the classroom emphasizes the wonder of living things as they are, not as they appear in fantasy. Books and other resources must be accurate in their portrayal of living things. As children begin to record what they see, fantasy will have its place, but should be clearly distinguished from reality. Conversations about their work can search for evidence and lead to comparisons that help children replace naïve notions with more accurate ideas.

---

2. **USE VIGNETTE 1 TO ILLUSTRATE THESE POINTS** (30 minutes). Introduce the vignette saying that they will be viewing the vignette they saw in basic workshop 1 again. Ask them to note the specific environmental and interaction strategies the teachers are using to create a culture of inquiry about nature.

Show the vignette and then ask for comments. Project overhead 7.1 while you talk. Guide teachers to identify specific strategies and note them on your chart. Connect each to the characteristic (from 7.1) to which the strategy relates. Be sure their ideas include both environment and interaction strategies.

Look for ideas like these:

- Teachers made specific comments to show respect for living things ("Don't squish him," "Be careful the stem doesn't break.").

- Teachers encourage close observation by using hand lenses and asking the children to talk about what they see.

- The teachers encourage children to share their theories by asking questions ("Where did the seed go? Where did the brown part go?") and listening attentively when the children share ideas (such as the interaction about the bug on the plant).

- Teacher has accurate resource materials available (such as the picture of the worm in the book and displayed on the wall).

- Displays reflect the children's work.

- Teachers observe and pursue children's interests and questions (such as the worm being tied up or the conversation based on an interest in snail movement).

- Data is gathered in varied ways: children drawing (with teacher support) and labeling, or the teacher documents what children find outdoors or what they say about snails.

- Conversations with individuals, small groups, and large groups—all provide vehicles for sharing observations and ideas.

- Teachers use open-ended questions ("Do you know what I was wondering . . . ? When the snail crawls on your arm, what did that feel like?"). Rephrase what children have said to encourage idea sharing ("Since worms don't have feet, it's okay to put water on them.").

- In all of the settings, actual plants and animals were used. Gummy worms have no place in this curriculum.

COMPLETE THE SELF-ASSESSMENT (35 MINUTES)

PURPOSE: While these key strategies are fresh in the teachers' minds, it will be important to help them think about the ones they need to build into their repertoire. This process will help you determine the content and form of professional development that will be most helpful to teachers right now.

1. **DISTRIBUTE "EVALUATING SCIENCE TEACHING"** to each teacher and ask them to take the next fifteen minutes to complete it. Emphasize the importance of openness. Remind the teachers that they all have strengths and weaknesses as teachers, but probably most are willing to acknowledge that science teaching is not a strength. Each teacher's ability to examine their own work will be the first step toward building the kind of reflective practice that will support their development as science teachers.

   While they work, move around the room seeing that everyone is on task. Help them interpret items that might confuse them.

2. **AFTER FIFTEEN MINUTES, ASK TEACHERS TO WORK IN SMALL GROUPS,** synthesizing their evaluation information (20 minutes). Help teachers divide into groups of three or four and

give each group a "Small Group Synthesis Form." Review the questions. Ask them to have a conversation and note their thoughts on the form as they talk. Suggest they have a note taker as well as someone who facilitates the conversation, ensuring they address all of the questions in the allotted time.

CONDUCT COLLECTIVE GOAL SETTING (15 MINUTES)

PURPOSE: This is an opportunity for you to collect some "data." Where do these teachers see their strengths and needs? Your responsiveness to their needs and interests will generate enthusiasm.

1. **BEGIN THE CONVERSATION BY FOCUSING ON THEIR STRENGTHS** (5 minutes). Quickly let each group share their thinking. In any group, the strengths and needs will vary from teacher to teacher, but look for themes, as well as for teachers who can support others in particular areas. Note their thoughts on the chart you prepared. You will want to refer to this information later.

2. **NOW GATHER THEIR THOUGHTS ABOUT THEIR NEEDS** (10 minutes). Repeat the process. Be sure each group has a chance to share. If you have time, encourage them to think about the next steps. You might want to offer alternatives, such as attending workshops, participating in guided discussions, and mentoring. Finish by letting teachers know what they might expect and reiterate your expectations for their use of the curriculum.

Suggested Next Steps

- Make a handout of the strategies teachers listed and distribute it.

- Offer workshops that best address the teachers' needs and interests.

- Design guided discussions that best address the teachers' needs and interests.

- Meet with each teacher individually to go over their evaluation, set goals, and make professional development plans. See the mentoring section for suggestions. We recommend that you conduct an observation in each room and fill out your own evaluation form before meeting with individual teachers.

- Suggest reading from the references:

  "Creating an Environment for Science in the Classroom," chapter 2 in *Doing What Scientists Do: Children Learn to Investigate Their World,* by E. Doris (Heinemann, 1991).

SMALL GROUP SYNTHESIS FORM

As a group, share your individual thoughts about your strengths and needs, and record them below. Note where there was common agreement and where there was a lot of difference.

Our strengths as science teachers include:

Our needs as science teachers include:

Areas we would like to develop first:

Deepening Children's Science Understandings

AT A GLANCE

Purpose:

- Build understanding of the strategies teachers can use to deepen science understandings as children engage in inquiry
- Apply these strategies to design next steps for the teacher featured in the video vignette

Activity	Time	Materials
Provide overview of how young children learn science Provide a rationale for this teaching approach by discussing how young children learn science.	20 minutes	• Overhead projector, screen, and overheads 8.1–8.4
Identify strategies for deepening children's science understandings Use excerpts from a teacher's journal to identify strategies for deepening children's science understandings. Reinforce ideas about the transition from open to focused exploration that were introduced in the basic workshops.	25 minutes	• Overhead 5.3 • Chart: "Strategies for Deepening Children's Science Understandings"
Analyze Vignette Ask teachers to analyze the strategies used by the teacher in the video vignette. In small groups, ask teachers to develop the next steps the teacher might take.	45 minutes	• Overhead 1.2 • VCR, monitor, and video cued to vignette 4: "Focused Exploration of Worms" • Copies of transcript for vignette 4, vignette observation form, and small group planning task

Pre-assignment: Read "The Teacher's Role" in resources (see p. 115) and "Worm City: Excerpts from a Teacher's Journal (see p. 10), both in the teacher's guide. Complete reflection questions.

Advanced Workshop 8:
Deepening Children's Science Understandings

OBJECTIVES

- Build understanding of the strategies teachers can use to deepen science understandings as children engage in inquiry

- Apply these strategies and design next steps for the teacher featured in the video vignette

OVERVIEW

- Provide overview of how young children learn science (20 minutes)

- Identify strategies for deepening children's science understandings (25 minutes)

- Analyze video vignette (40 minutes)

INSTRUCTOR PREPARATION

- **ASSIGN "READ AND REFLECT."** Distribute "Read and Reflect 8" at least one week before the workshop.

- **PREVIEW VIGNETTE 4: "FOCUSED EXPLORATION OF WORMS."** Watch the vignette and understand how it illustrates the points you want to make.

MATERIALS

- Overhead projector, screen, and overheads 1.2, 5.3, and 8.1–8.4

- VCR, monitor, and video cued to vignette 4: "Focused Exploration of Worms"

- Copies of handouts: transcript of vignette 4, vignette observation form, and "Read and Reflect 8"

- Chart: "Strategies for Deepening Children's Science Understandings," with two sections ("Encourage Exploration" and "Deepen Science Understanding")

Activity

OVERVIEW OF HOW YOUNG CHILDREN LEARN SCIENCE (20 MINUTES)

PURPOSE: To set the stage for the content that follows, building the connection between inquiry and its role in science learning with what we know about how young children learn.

1. **INTRODUCE THE WORKSHOP** and provide a quick overview of the main goals of an inquiry-based teacher (5 minutes). After introducing the topic of the workshop, show overhead 8.1: "The Science Teacher's Goals." Emphasize that the focus here is inquiry science and that this workshop will focus on the second and third goals—how teachers can guide children's inquiry and deepen children's science understandings. Mention that this might seem

obvious, but in practice it is very difficult and these workshops are all designed to help them accomplish these goals.

OVERHEAD 8.1: THE SCIENCE TEACHER'S GOALS

- **Encourage children's discovery of the natural world**
- **Guide children's inquiry**
- **Deepen children's science understanding**

---

2. **PROVIDE OVERVIEW OF HOW CHILDREN LEARN SCIENCE** (20 minutes) using overhead 8.2. Make the point that the inquiry approach to teaching science is based on what we know about the nature of science, as well as what we know about how children learn. Use the references to excerpts from a teacher's journal to illustrate the points, or ask your teachers if they can make these connections.

OVERHEAD 8.2: SCIENCE TEACHING AND LEARNING

- **Young children develop ideas about science from their life experiences**
  Alyssa said the wind blew the chimes. Eddie said that the worms were dead because they were shot. The children suggested that worms eat leaves, chocolate, and ice cream. Children often relate observations of animals to their own lives. If they like ice cream so do worms or the longest worm is the daddy—these are examples of ideas that children have formed based on what they know already about the world.

- **New experiences lead children to challenge previous naïve ideas**
  If the teacher structures an investigation about what worms eat and children observe them over a few days in their natural habitat, they will find that a worm's diet is different from their own and are more likely to give up the notion that worms eat chocolate and ice cream. This is likely to happen over time, not immediately. Correcting children verbally does not have the same power as providing new information through experiences.

- **A balance between exploration and thinking, reasoning, and theorizing provides a strong basis for learning**
  The excerpts from a teacher's journal provide a picture of how this balance plays out over time. Repeated patterns of doing and talking can deepen children's understanding over time. When the teacher encourages inquiry, lifelong patterns for learning are established.

- **Inquiry that leads to science learning takes time**
  These journal entries provide an excellent example of the kind of time it takes for children to build new understandings through inquiry. The quality of the children's inquiry deepens with time. For example, the October 16 investigation of what worms eat was more complex than the one on September 8.

- **With guidance, children have the ability to engage in all aspects of the inquiry process**
  Note in the journal entries that children question, conduct investigations, use tools, communicate their ideas, and make reasonable explanations, but the teacher plays a key role in guiding this process.

---

3. CONCLUDE BY MAKING KEY POINTS ABOUT THIS APPROACH (5 minutes). Use 8.3 and 8.4 to focus your comments.

OVERHEAD 8.3: KEY IDEAS ABOUT THIS APPROACH TO SCIENCE LEARNING

- **Building understanding of important science concepts is an appropriate goal for young children**
It is clear, from the vignettes and from the children's work samples that were included in the workshops and teacher's guide, that young children are capable of learning science.

- **Children naturally form ideas about the world based on their life experiences**
The vignettes are full of examples of children's ideas about how the world works. They draw on their immediate life experiences to create these theories.

- **In inquiry-based science our role is to provide new experiences that can lead children to more sophisticated theories.**
Our goal is to provide new experiences that will contribute to the development of new, more reasoned understandings. In particular, we hope children will begin to use evidence (what they have observed) as they build their ideas of how the world works.

OVERHEAD 8.4:

"Experience is not the best teacher. It sounds like heresy, but when you think about it, it's reflection on experience that makes it educational."

George Forman
Professor Emeritus, University of Massachusetts

As teachers view 8.4, explain that you will help them think about their role in providing the right experiences, helping children focus on the science in those experiences, and guiding a meaningful reflection process.

IDENTIFY STRATEGIES FOR DEEPENING CHILDREN'S SCIENCE UNDERSTANDINGS (25 MINUTES)

PURPOSE: The analysis of excerpts from a teachers journal will highlight strategies teachers can use to promote children's science understandings.

1. ANALYZE EXCERPTS FROM A TEACHER'S JOURNAL TO IDENTIFY STRATEGIES (15 minutes).
Ask teachers for strategies they found in the journal entries, noting their responses on the chart you have prepared. Use the question about literacy and math to highlight where science provides opportunities to promote learning early literacy and math concepts. Ask for specifics about what the journal says and connect it to the strategy they have identified.

An important point: deeper understandings grow out of reflection but they are only possible with carefully focused experiences that happen over time. Look for strategies like these:

Encourage children's exploration:

- Worked with small groups during open exploration (September 18)
- Used observations to identify children's interests (October 4)
- Created indoor home for worms so children could look for their basic needs (October 10)
- Provided materials for and encouraged representation of worms and leaves (October 11)
- Called attention to worm movement during observation (October 12)
- Involved children in planning investigation of what worms eat (October 16)
- Prepared indoor and outdoor environments that stimulate inquiry.

Deepen children's science understandings:

- Facilitated large group science talk to share what we have found (September 23)
- Offered her developing theory about this learning process (September 30)
- Asked how children knew worms weren't alive, which offered an opportunity to share theories (October 11)
- Used representations to focus children's observations (October 11)
- Documented children's ideas about what worms eat (October 12)

Supported literacy and math development:

The teacher built children's capacity to use language to express their ideas, which is key to early literacy. Children cannot learn to read and write if they do not have an understanding of language.

- On October 1, the children counted the worms. In science this is data collection, but it is also math.
- On October 4, the children measured worms, an important math concept.
- On October 11, children drew worms and leaves. This form of symbolic representation is important to literacy development.
- On October 16, the teacher mentioned bringing in nonfiction books. This provides an important purpose for reading—children are motivated to find information by reading about the plants and animals they are observing.

2. **DISCUSS THE TRANSITION FROM OPEN EXPLORATION TO FOCUSED EXPLORATION** (10 minutes). Spend a few minutes reviewing overhead 5.3 and talking about the transition from open exploration to focused exploration. Use journal excerpts and teacher's classroom observations (examples in box below) to illustrate how children show their readiness to focus.

   a. Review overhead 5.3 from basic workshop 5.

OVERHEAD 5.3: THE TRANSITION FROM OPEN EXPLORATION TO FOCUSED EXPLORATION

Look for children doing the following:

- **Observing the same plant or animal from one day to the next**
  For example, you will see children returning to an outdoor site or the terrarium repeatedly. They may connect their observations from one day to the next, or they may begin to ask questions about their observations.

- **Examining a particular aspect or characteristic of a living thing**
  For example, children may show interest in how an animal eats or how quickly a plant grows or what it looks like underground.

- **Finding photos or information in books about plants or animals they observed**
  They may want to identify a plant or animal, learning its name or finding out some fact, such as how many legs an animal has or what it eats.

Look for connections to the journal entries like these:

- Observing the same plant or animal from one day to the next—On October 4 the teacher noticed that some children are particularly interested in worms.

- Examining a particular aspect or characteristic of a living thing—There is evidence of this in several places, but the October 4 entry is what triggered the teacher to begin a focused exploration. At this point, the children showed an interest in the characteristics and behaviors of worms by measuring, drawing, and thinking about how they move.

---

b. If you have time, encourage teachers to share their classroom observations, pinpointing readiness to shift to focused exploration, or alternately, children who are not ready to make the shift. Time won't permit everyone to share, but you will want to keep the conversation going until you have a variety of examples and you think everyone has a clear understanding of child behavior that shows a readiness for focused investigation. Find an opportunity to remind teachers that they will not hurt children by hurrying them. If a child isn't ready, she will let the teacher know.

ANALYSIS OF VIGNETTE (40 MINUTES)

PURPOSE: Analyzing classroom practice will help teachers make the transition from theory to practice. While the vignette shows one point in time, this activity will put these isolated events into a context of inquiry that will build over the course of days and weeks.

1. **READ THE STRATEGIES LISTED ON THE POSTER** (5 minutes). Ask teachers if they have anything to add after reading the section on the teacher's role. Add their specific strategies to the list. Suggest that they can look for these strategies in the vignette, as well as add new ones.

2. **USE VIGNETTE 4 TO FURTHER DISCUSS HOW TO DEEPEN SCIENCE UNDERSTANDINGS** (20 minutes). Begin by noting that this vignette was filmed in the same classroom as in vignette 3 in basic workshop 5. It is a Boston Head Start classroom with twenty three- and

four-year-olds. Teachers will see a group of five boys who are observing worms. These children are all English language learners. Their first languages are Farsi, Arabic, Serbo-Croatian, and Ibo. (Below find guidance for discussing the strategies the teacher is using to support these second language learners.) Pass out the vignette observation form and tell teachers that you want them to notice the ways the teacher encourages inquiry in order to deepen children's science understandings. As you discuss their observations, put new strategies in the appropriate column ("Encourage Exploration" and "Deepen Science Understanding"). Ask teachers of second language learners to look for these strategies as well.

Look for ideas such as the following:

What is important about these strategies is the way the teacher calls the children's attention to the characteristics of the worm, focusing them on the science. Strategies include the following:

- Putting worms on the table for close observation

- Referring to the book to compare the band around the worm

- Asking questions ("What do you see? Where is the worm going? Do you think it will go to the edge of the table? What makes you think that is his head?")

- Sharing her own observations ("Look how far it went, Hussein. It started moving really fast, didn't it. It's bigger than that one.")

- Helping children communicate through movement as well as words

- Using children's names to draw them into the exploration

English Language Learning Strategies

This teacher uses a variety of strategies to support English language learners as they try to communicate their observations and ideas. These strategies include the following:

- Using Ikechukwu's name regularly, which includes him in the exploration

- Accepting Aria's use of movement to communicate his ideas, then putting them into words for him

- Rephrasing and correcting their errors ("He tied himself up?" rather than "hisself")

- Using key vocabulary words along with movements (for example, "stretching," "pulling")

---

3. **DISCUSS THE NEXT STEPS THE TEACHER MIGHT MAKE** to expand the children's inquiry (15 minutes). Put the inquiry diagram on the overhead projector (overhead 1.2). Point to the circle that illustrates the cyclical nature of inquiry in focused exploration saying you want them to think about this aspect of inquiry as they plan strategies for deepening children's science understanding. Use the following questions to guide a discussion:

   - What were children's interests and questions?

     – The band (the *clitellum*) that made the worm appear "tied up," worm movement, comparative size

   - What science concepts are these interests related to? What science are we deepening?

     – Characteristics of worms—physical (the band on the worm, comparative size) and behavioral (how they move, their speed)

- How might the teacher use inquiry to deepen understanding about one or more of these science concepts? (You might pick one to focus on, then move on to another if there is time.) Taking movement as an example, here are some ideas:

  - Note predictions for what the worms would do when they reached the edge of the table, and then note what actually happened with several worms. Analyze this data, thinking about what it means. Why do the children think the worms behaved as they did?

  - Map their movement on paper following their trail (perhaps you could put up some barriers and see what they do). Have the children describe what the worms have done and why they might be moving the way they are. Again, encourage analysis with questions: "Why this direction? How are they sensing what is ahead?"

If you are going to investigate comparative size, do activities like these:

- Measure a variety of worms and make a chart of the measurements. Use pieces of string or a ruler to measure. Keep in mind that a worm's length can change depending on whether or not it is moving.

- If you can distinguish worms by identifiable characteristics, measure a set of worms over time looking for growth.

- Note relative "fatness" and encourage children to represent these variations in their drawings or clay work.

If the focus is on the characteristics of worms, such as the band around them, do activities like these:

- Encourage descriptive language as children compare one worm to others.

- Use various two- and three-dimensional media to represent the features that children notice.

- Use books and Web sites to learn about the function of body parts after the children have developed and shared their own theories.

Emphasize that deepening children's science understandings can't happen in one day, but can take place over a week or two. Remind your teachers of the importance of documentation so they can build on children's experiences from one day to the next. For example, use children's representations of worms as a springboard for discussion—focus on the parts of the worm they have been drawing and each part's purpose.

In closing, encourage teachers to continue sharing what they are doing in their classrooms. Remind them when and where the next workshop or guided discussion is and what they need to do to prepare.

Suggested Next Steps

- Make a handout of the strategies teachers have listed and distribute it.

- Follow up with teachers: Ask if they have any issues with focused exploration or with their role as a facilitator of inquiry. You may ask, "What are children's current interests and questions? How do they show these?"

Do teachers find ways to help children collect and record their data and talk about what it means?

- Offer the workshops on science talks or on representation as a way of extending the conversation about inquiry and deepening understanding.

- Guide a few discussions on these concepts. Take video vignettes into teachers' rooms to use for discussion. Help them consider next steps and plan ways to support how children collect and analyze data.

- Suggest readings from the references:

Cooperative Problem Solving in the Classroom: Enhancing Young Children's Cognitive Development, by Jonathan Trudge and David Caruso (NAEYC, 1988)

Using Photographs to Support Children's Science Inquiry, by Cynthia Hoisington (NAEYC, 2002)

Transcript of Video Vignette 4:
Focused Exploration of Worms

Scene: Five children—Ikechukwu *(green shirt)*, Aria *(white shirt)*, Roney *(plaid shirt)*, Hussein *(red shirt)*, and Ervin *(striped shirt)* are observing worms on a table.

Teacher: We have to find Ikechukwu a worm and Daphne a worm. Daphne, look in here. There's two more worms.

Teacher: Do you want to look at the worms with the magnifying glass? Look. Look, here. *(Gives hand lens to child)* Aria, let Hussein look too.

Aria: *(Puts hand lens over worm)* Hey, Cindy, look!

Teacher: What do you see?

Aria: It looks big. He tied hisself.

Teacher: He tied himself up? Is that what it looks like? That thing around him. Do you remember something like that in this book? It showed that part. Look at the part that looks like it's tied up. Do you see it in the pictures? Look, Roney.

Aria: Yah.

Teacher: *(Puts book on table)* Did you see this part on the worm? Look at the worm. See if you can see that part on the worm. Ikechukwu . . . Let's move it over for Ikechukwu.

(Ikechukwu looks at book with magnifying glass.)

Teacher: Do you see it, Roney? See that part. Ikechukwu, what do you see?

(Ikechukwu studying worm with magnifying glass)

Teacher: Roney, do you know what? I don't want you to climb on the table. Roney, did you get it wet?

Roney: Yah.

Teacher: Where's the worm going, Ikechukwu?

Aria: Cindy, you can't put water on this kind of bug. Maybe it can't move. *(Aria is motioning with arms.)* It's kind of *(inaudible)* slippery.

Teacher: Oh, I didn't think about that because we put water on the worms, but maybe we can't put water on other kinds.

Aria: Because that one has feet because *(inaudible)* his feet slip.

Teacher: Because worms don't have feet, it's okay to put water on them. But because that kind has feet, the water makes his feet go slip. So you think maybe we better not put water on it.

(Teacher and children are observing worm on table.)

Teacher: Where's it going? Where's it going, Hussein?

Teacher: *(To another child)* This one's not moving as much as the other one.

(Child puts hand on table near where worm is crawling, as if to stop it.)

Child: Look, it's scared.

Teacher: Where's it going, Hussein? Look at how far it went, Hussein. Do you remember it was here *(pointing)* and it went all the way there. It went far. Do you think it will go to the edge of the table?

(Two boys—Roney with a magnifying glass and Hussein with a pitcher—are observing the same worm using their instruments to create barriers.)

Teacher: What happened, Roney? Did you bump it by accident? Wow, he started moving really fast, didn't it. He didn't like that I don't think. What's it doing now?

(Hussein takes water pitcher and puts it near worm.)

Teacher: You know what, Hussein? We really want to watch the worm right now. If you want to put some water on it, you can use the spray bottle.

Teacher: *(Observing another worm)* Look at this one. Look at how long it is.

Roney: That one's big.

Teacher: That one's big isn't it?

Child: *(Inaudible)*

Teacher: It's bigger than that one.

Ikechukwu: *(Inaudible)*

Teacher: That's right. When it wants to move . . . we read about that. Right? How does it move?

Ikechukwu: He *(inaudible)* his head like that.

Teacher: Oh, he slips himself? What about what you were saying about stretching and pulling in, stretching and pulling in. Is that what it's doing now?

Ikechukwu: *(Inaudible)* like a snake.

Teacher: Like a snake? Can you show me with your body?

Hussein: Look, it's bigger.

Aria: *(Puts his hand on the worm and moves it back and forth)* That's how he moves hisself.

Teacher: It kind of goes back and forth?

Child: You see how it goes?

Teacher: Hussein, Ari is talking about the way the worm's moving.

Aria: It moves and goes like that. *(Hand gestures over worm.)*

Teacher: You mean he pulls this part front first and pulls the back part in? What's going to happen when it gets to the edge of the table I wonder? Do you think it will fall, Ikechukwu?

Child: It's going to fall down. *(Puts hand at edge of table.)*

Teacher: Do you think it will fall, Roney? It's going to fall down? Move your hand, move your hand. Let's see what happens. We won't let it fall down.

Aria: *(Points to worm)* This is his head and this is his tail.

Teacher: What makes you think that's his head?

Aria: Because he moves that side.

Teacher: Because he moves that side first.

ADVANCED WORKSHOP 8: VIGNETTE OBSERVATION FORM

Note your observations by identifying the teacher strategies and child responses in separate columns.

Child Behavior/Comments	Teacher Response

READ AND REFLECT 8

Name: _____

Before coming to workshop 8: "Deepening Children's Science Understandings," read about the teacher's role in "Resources" (p. 115) and excerpts from a teacher's journal (p. 10), both in the teacher's guide. Respond to these questions as you reflect on what you read.

1. In what ways did the teacher in the excerpts from a teacher's journal encourage the children's exploration? What strategies did she use? Note exactly what she did and the date of the entry.

2. In what ways did the teacher deepen children's science understanding? What strategies did she use? Note exactly what she did and the date of the entry.

3. In what ways did the teacher promote early math and literacy learning? What strategies did she use? Note exactly what she did and the date of the entry.

Using Books to Extend Science Learning

AT A GLANCE

Purpose:

- Learn how to select books and use them to enrich children's exploration of nature
- Learn to use field guides during outdoor explorations

Activity	Time	Materials
Examine use of books to enrich the children's exploration of nature Guide teachers as they examine different categories of books and consider the varied ways books can enrich children's investigations.	45 minutes	• Sample books • Copies of "Small Group Discussion about Books" • Chart: "Different Categories of Books"
Use field guides during outdoor explorations Guide teachers as they use field guides in a brief outdoor exploration.	45 minutes	• Penlights and hand lenses for small group (optional) • Field guides

Pre-assignment: Have teachers bring books they have been using that are related to exploring nature. Read the sections on extensions and books and media in the teacher's guide (see p. 130).

Advanced Workshop 9:
Using Books to Extend Science Learning

Objectives

- Learn how to select books and use them to enrich children's exploration of nature
- Learn how to use field guides during outdoor explorations

Overview

- Examine use of books to enrich the children's exploration of nature (45 minutes)
- Use field guides during outdoor exploration (45 minutes)

Instructor Preparation

- **Give assignment to teachers.** At least a week before the workshop, tell teachers you want them to read the sections on extensions and books and media in the teacher's guide, and to bring a few (three to five) books they have been using in their naturalist exploration.
- **Select appropriate field guides.** Be sure the field guides reflect what teachers might observe when they are outdoors. Trees and birds are possibilities.

Materials

- Three to four books from each of the following categories (Note: See pp. 130–135 of the teacher's guide for a list of recommended books within each category.)
- Field guides (Proved a variety for comparison. Each small group will need one.)
    - Informational books
    - Image books
    - Fiction books
    - Biographies
    - Poetry books
- Copies of handout: "Small Group Discussion about Books"
- Chart: "Different Categories of Books"

Activity

Examine Use of Books to Enrich Children's Exploration of Nature (1 hour 5 minutes)

Purpose: This activity will help participants identify ways they can use different kinds of books to enrich children's exploration of nature. It is also important to note how this activity promotes children's literacy development. When children are highly motivated by their science investigations, they easily learn the value of books as a resource, while at the same time they learn how to use books.

1. **ASK PARTICIPANTS TO SHARE BOOKS** they have used as part of their exploration of nature (15 minutes). Open by mentioning the importance of books—their value to literacy development and science learning. Focus the discussion on how teachers chose these books and how they have been used. You might ask, "When did you introduce these books and why?" "How did you use these books with children?" "What did you accomplish?"

2. **DISCUSS TYPES OF BOOKS THEY CAN USE** (30 minutes).

   a. Ask participants to turn to p. 130 of the teacher's guide, which describes different types of books that enrich children's naturalist explorations. Review the different categories with participants. Use books teachers brought in as examples for each category.

   b. Ask participants to form small groups of three or four. Give each group several books, all from the same category (so one group will have information books and others will have real-life fiction). Also distribute the handout: "Small Group Discussion about Books." Ask groups to look through their books, then use the questions on the handout to discuss how they might use this type of book with children. Note: One person in each group should record the discussion. Allow fifteen minutes for this small group exploration of books.

   c. Bring the whole group together. Ask one person from each group to share key points that were raised during their small group discussions.

You may want to highlight the following points during the whole group debriefing:

- There are different types of books that teachers can use with children to extend their exploration of living things. Some of these books, such as picture books, are usually read cover to cover. In contrast, children may only look at select pages of information books, carefully observing images or finding needed information.

- Nonfiction books should all be scientifically accurate, engaging, and informative for young children. Fiction books are not always accurate. When reading or looking at books with children, help them connect what they see in books to their own direct experiences outdoors and in the classroom.

- Teachers can make a special effort to display books that have engaging pictures of the plants and animals children have been observing.

- Teachers sometimes have difficulty finding a place for fiction books in a nature exploration. Suggest they use books to deepen children's understanding of a scientific idea. For example, they might read *The Very Hungry Caterpillar* and discuss how the story differs from children's experiences with real animals.

Conclude by reviewing the different categories of books that appear on pp. 130–135 of the teacher's guide. Suggest that participants use the list of recommended books, choosing from each of the categories to enrich their exploration.

Use Field Guides During an Outdoor Exploration (45 minutes)

Purpose: Through direct experience, teachers will learn about the importance of field guides and ways to use them with children.

1. **Introduce participants to the field guides** they will use during a brief outdoor exploration (5 minutes). Explain that field guides are an important type of book to use during their outdoor explorations. These guides are critical, helping naturalists identify the names of plants and animals and their unique characteristics. Distribute the field guides that teachers will share, then take them outdoors for a twenty-five-minute exploration. Suggest they identify one or two of their favorite findings. The field guides will encourage examination of details—so you might also want to give them penlights and hand lenses.

2. **During the outdoor exploration, encourage the teachers to use the field guides** (25 minutes):

   - Share your curiosity about what the guide might say: "I wonder if the guide says something about the habits of that bird?"

   - Model use of the guide by noticing similarities or differences in a particular organism.

   - Guide teachers beyond the picture to the information about an organism they are examining.

> Be sure to emphasize that plant and animal identification is not the goal. Rather, having children compare pictures to actual plants and animals and noticing important characteristics are critical.

3. **Bring teachers together to discuss their experience** (15 minutes)
   Begin by asking the following:

   - What did you find?

   - How was the field guide helpful?

   - What types of information did it give you?

   Then apply this experience to their work with children. Ask, "How might you use field guides with children to enrich their exploration of nature?"

> Look for ideas like these:
>
> - Put guides with the tools the children take outdoors.
>
> - Suggest children look up a plant or animal they are interested in.
>
> - Ask questions that focus children's observation while using the guides, for example, "Does the bush in the picture have the same shaped leaves as the bush you are observing? Does the animal have the same number of legs?"
>
> - Provide vocabulary, but remember that the real purpose is to heighten observation skills and recognize the field guide as a tool.

In conclusion, let teachers know when and where the next training activity will be.

Suggested Next Steps

- If you want to further pursue the ways that inquiry-based science promotes literacy development, you might offer the representation workshops.

- Plan guided discussions that provide an opportunity for teachers to further share their experiences with books.

- Conduct observations of teachers when they are using books. Have a follow-up conference, helping teachers examine their practice.

- Suggest readings from the references:

Learning to Read and Write: Developmentally Appropriate Practices for Young Children, by the National Association for the Education of Young Children (NAEYC, 1998)

Taking Inquiry Outdoors: Reading, Writing, and Science Beyond the Classroom Walls, by Barbara Bourne (Stenhouse, 2000)

Nature, Literature, and Young Children: A Natural Combination, by Barbara N. Kupetz and Meghan N. Twiest (NAEYC, 2000)

SMALL GROUP DISCUSSION ABOUT BOOKS

Use these questions to guide your small group discussion.

1. What are the special features of this type of book (such as, provides accurate information, photos offer realistic images, and so on)?

2. When would you use this type of book with children?

3. How might you use this type of book to enrich children's explorations of nature?

4. How might you use books? (Such as during small group science talks? Outdoor explorations?)

5. What do you think are some of the benefits of using this type of book with children (namely, what can children gain)?

6. Is the book scientifically accurate? If not, how would you deal with that?

Assessing Children's Science Learning

AT A GLANCE

Purpose:

- Become familiar with the assessment tools in the teacher's guide
- Practice using the observation records and plan for their systematic use

Activity	Time	Materials
Provide overview of assessment tools in the teacher's guide Offer a framework for assessing children's science learning—its purpose and the process	15 minutes	• Overhead projector, screen, and overhead 10.1
Conduct observation of young naturalists at work Use the observation record form to assess children's science learning	45 minutes	• Chart: "Observing Young Naturalists" • VCR, monitor, and video vignette 4: "Focused Exploration of Worms" • Copies of observation record
Relate to teachers' practices Discuss ways teachers can systematically use the observation record and the learning record to regularly assess children's inquiry skills and science understandings.	30 minutes	

Pre-assignment: Read the "Observation and Assessment" section in the teacher's guide (see p. 119). Use the observation record in the teacher's guide to document what children say and do during an exploration of nature.

Advanced Workshop 10: Assessing Children's Science Learning

OBJECTIVES

- Become familiar with the assessment tools in the teacher's guide
- Practice using the observation records and plan for their systematic use

OVERVIEW

- Overview of assessment tools in the teacher's guide (15 minutes)
- Practice observing young naturalists at work (45 minutes)
- Relate assessment practices to own teaching practice (30 minutes)

INSTRUCTOR PREPARATION

- **REVIEW VIGNETTE 4: "FOCUSED EXPLORATION OF WORMS."** View it and note the aspects that you will highlight during the workshop. This video vignette is also used in advanced workshop 8.

MATERIALS

- Chart: "Observing Young Naturalists"
- VCR, monitor, and video cued to vignette 4: "Focused Exploration of Worms"
- Overhead projector, screen, and overhead 10.1
- Copies of transcript for vignette 4 and an observation record for each teacher

Activity

OVERVIEW OF ASSESSMENT IN SCIENCE EXPLORATIONS (15 MINUTES)

PURPOSE: This activity will set the stage for those that follow by proving an assessment framework for science learning, its purpose and process.

1. **INTRODUCE THE WORKSHOP AND DISCUSS THE PURPOSE OF ASSESSMENT** (5 minutes). Give an overview of the activities. Ask teachers why they think assessment is important and what it involves. Allow them to share their ideas, reinforcing those that refer to assessment as a way to make informed decisions about teaching and learning. Emphasize these points:

   - Assessment provides information about children's interests, abilities, and understandings.
   - Ultimately, the teacher learns about the effectiveness of her teaching through assessment.
   - Assessment is ongoing and the process includes documentation, reflection, and planning.

2. INTRODUCE THE KEY ELEMENTS OF THE ASSESSMENT PROCESS USING OVERHEAD 10.1 (5 minutes).

Key Elements of Assessment Process

- Collecting data

  You might want to ask teachers what they think data means in this context. Emphasize the value of regularly collecting multiple sources of data (written observations, photographs, video and audio tape, or samples of children's work) that can provide insights about children's inquiry skills and their understandings of the science concepts. Suggest that teachers document at least one observation per child every two weeks, and collect one work sample per child per week.

- Analyzing data regularly

  This data will only have meaning when teachers take time to think about it. Teachers should examine varied documents to gauge each child's engagement and science learning. At the same time, teachers should look at the class as a whole and where it is going.

- Drawing conclusions and making decisions

  Conclusions are about the important links between teaching and learning. Are children engaged? Are they deepening their understanding of the science concepts by using inquiry? Are all children making progress? What does this mean for your teaching? These are the key questions that will lead to conclusions and making informed decisions about next steps.

---

3. ASK TEACHERS TO OPEN THEIR TEACHER'S GUIDES to "Science Outcomes: Science Inquiry Skills and Science Concepts" (5 minutes) in the appendices (pp. 147–148). Review the chart with them, pointing out the kinds of information it provides. Explain that they will use this chart as a basis for assessing children's science learning.

PRACTICE USING THE OBSERVATION RECORD (45 MINUTES)

PURPOSE: This activity will help teachers learn what to look for as they observe and document their observations using the Observation Record Form. Such an activity will help teachers focus on science concepts and inquiry skills as they assess children's learning.

1. OBSERVE AND DISCUSS VIGNETTE 4: "FOCUSED EXPLORATION OF WORMS" (45 minutes).

  a. Start by asking the teachers what they look for as they assess their children's engagement and understandings. Note their ideas on the chart, "Observing Young Naturalists." Add important ideas that they do not mention.

Look for ideas such as whether or not the children are showing interest and staying with an activity, the aspects of inquiry they are using, the ways they are communicating ideas, the ideas they have, the science concepts they are exploring, and the quality of their interaction with other children.

---

  b. Introduce vignette 4 by saying that this vignette was filmed in a Boston Head Start classroom. They will observe a group of five boys between the age of three and four who focused on worms and have some in a terrarium. These children are all English language learners. Their first languages are Farsi, Arabic, Serbo-Croatian, and Ibo. Tell them they will be watching the vignette twice; the second time they will take notes.

c. Show the vignette. Then ask teachers what they noticed about the children's engagement and their understandings. Listen to their comments, asking for specifics and keeping teachers focused on what they actually saw, not their interpretation of it. For example, they may notice Roney doesn't use much language. They shouldn't assume that he has a language delay. Highlight any differences of opinion or questions.

d. Prepare for the next viewing by passing out the observation record and transcript and telling teachers the names of the children. Beginning on the right back side of the table and moving clockwise, they are Ervin, Ikechukwu, Hussein (on the end), Roney, and Aria. Remind them that their notes should be objective—not interpretations. Also encourage them to use the outcomes chart to focus their observations.

e. Show the vignette again. Then ask teachers what they noticed this time. During the conversation, highlight important aspects of documenting observations:

- Document—Complete and objective notes are critical. Have some teachers tell the class what they wrote. You might want to take one small sequence and get a couple of variations, working toward a more complete statement. (Mention that this is similar to one major goal for the children—to observe and describe what they see.)

- Analyze—Consider the variations in children's engagement and understandings that come when you begin to interpret the observation notes. Reflecting on what children say and do provides insights into their level of engagement and their science understandings. In this vignette, all of the children are attentively watching the worms. Aria is fairly articulate as he shares his theory about water on bugs. His words and actions demonstrate that he is thinking about the needs and characteristics of bugs and worms, as well as their behaviors.

- Plan—Observations can help teachers plan next steps. For example, children's curiosity about worm size and how they move could lead to further investigations.

Discuss Own Classroom Observations (30 minutes)

Purpose: This is an opportunity for the teachers to connect their new understandings about assessment to their own classroom practice. They can also look for ways to incorporate the assessment tools into their ongoing work.

1. **Conduct an informal conversation** (20 minutes). Ask teachers how they have connected this approach to their own assessment practices. Use the following questions to focus their comments: (Continue to refer to the outcomes chart.)

   - What kind of science engagement do you see in your classroom? Let teachers talk about what they are seeing for a few minutes. Then ask them to examine the science concepts (noted on the outcomes chart) being explored and the inquiry their children are engaged in.

   - In what ways have you recorded your observations? For instance, teachers may place clipboards around the room with copies of the observation form so they are always available. Also, encourage use of multimedia, including audio and tape recording, because such methods capture moments that allow for deeper reflection. Elicit issues teachers have with the process and encourage them to help each other resolve barriers they encounter. For example, talk about how they might use the observation records regularly.

- Are you systematically analyzing your data? Find out when they are finding time for reflection, letting them learn from each other. Allow issues to surface and help teachers find solutions. Be sure they understand that observations and other documents become more valuable if it is used for assessment purposes, informing teaching on a regular basis.

2. **INTRODUCE THE OBSERVATION RECORD** (10 minutes) by asking them to turn to p. 143 in their teacher's guides. Explain that this is a way of recording science inquiry and understandings over the period of one exploration. Mention that the outcomes will help them with the meaning of some of these items. Use Aria as an example and ask what might be noted about him based on this one observation. While you cannot distinguish "sometimes" and "consistently," you can identify things that he reveals about his understandings and inquiry skills. Look for ideas such as how he explores or questions, collects and synthesizes data, and uses language to communicate findings. He has some understanding of the characteristics of living things and their needs, and of diversity and variation.

Conclude by sharing the topic of the next professional development event and when it is scheduled. Give teachers any assignment you want them to complete in preparation.

Suggested Next Steps

- Follow up with individual teachers to see if they are finding ways to use the assessment tools in their classrooms. Key to their success with the tools is their ability to make sense of the science in their children's explorations. Look for any issues they might have with the science and provide support when needed. One strategy is to observe them and talk about the science. Another would be to view vignettes and just talk about the science understandings evident in each one.

- The representation and documentation panel workshops all reinforce ideas about assessment.

- Use upcoming guided discussions to examine and discuss what children's work samples and conversations reveal about their level of engagement, inquiry skills, and science understandings.

- Suggest readings from the references:

"The Role of the Constructivist Teacher," chapter 4 in *The Young Child as Scientist: A Constructivist Approach to Early Childhood Science Education,* by C. Chaille and L. Britain (Allyn & Bacon, 2003)

Learning in Science: The Implications of Children's Science, by R. Osborne and P. Freyberg (Heinemann, 1985)

Encouraging Representation

AT A GLANCE

Purpose:

- Gain an understanding of the purpose of observational drawing and other forms of representation in young children's science learning
- Identify strategies for encouraging representation
- Practice assessing children's representations
- Learn to select and display appropriate materials

Activity	Time	Materials
Provide an overview of the role of representation in inquiry science Use overheads to introduce this session and discuss how representation can promote children's science learning.	15 minutes	• Overhead projector, screen, and overhaeads 11.1–11.3
Discuss encouraging representation through conversation Use a video vignette to discuss the ways a teacher can support representation.	30 minutes	• VCR, monitor, and video cued to vignette 5: "Encouraging Representation" • Chart: "Strategies for Encouraging Representation" • Copies of vignette observation form and transcript of vignette 5
Discuss encouraging representation through the environment and routines Facilitate a conversation about appropriate representation materials and how to make them accessible to the children during their exploration. Share the importance of regular routines.	15 minutes	
Help teachers assess children's representations Guide teachers as they analyze overheads of children's work, using the document annotation form from the teacher's guide.	30 minutes	• Overheads 11.4–11.8 • Copies of document annotations

Pre-assignment: Review the section on representation in "The Teacher's Role," which appears on p. 115 of the teacher's guide.

Advanced Workshop 11: Encouraging Representation

OBJECTIVES

- Gain an understanding of the purpose of observational drawing and other forms of representation in young children's science learning
- Identify strategies for encouraging representation
- Practice assessing children's representations
- Learn to select and display appropriate materials

OVERVIEW

- Provide overview of the role of representation (15 minutes)
- Discuss encouraging representation through conversations (30 minutes)
- Discuss encouraging representation through the environment and routines (15 minutes)
- Help teachers assess children's representations (30 minutes)

INSTRUCTOR PREPARATION

- **GIVE ASSIGNMENT.** At least one week before the workshop ask teachers to review the section on representation that appears in "Resources" on p. 119 of the teacher's guide.
- **REVIEW VIGNETTE.** View the vignette and note teaching strategies that you will highlight in the workshop.

MATERIALS

- Copies of document annotations (p. 144 in the teacher's guide)
- Overhead projector, screen, and overheads 11.1–11.8
- VCR, monitor, and video cued to vignette 5: "Encouraging Representation"
- Chart: "Strategies for Encouraging Representation"
- Copies of vignette observation form and transcript of vignette 5 for each teacher

Activity

OVERVIEW OF THE ROLE OF REPRESENTATION (15 MINUTES)

PURPOSE: Understanding how representation can promote children's inquiry and science understandings will be key to the teachers' work with children. This overview will also set the stage for the rest of this workshop.

1. **INTRODUCE THE WORKSHOP AND PROVIDE AN OVERVIEW** of the purpose of representation in science teaching and learning (5 minutes). Provide an overview of the activities in this

workshop. Show overhead 11.1. Note that Sherri has done aerial views of her plants, showing leaves, stems, and the dirt in the pots. Her work shows what happens when children do observational drawing regularly. Use the following discussion points to talk about the purpose of representation:

- Encourages children to look closely at the characteristics of living things, their parts and their functions.

- Builds abilities to use multiple media to communicate observations and ideas.

- Encourages new questions.

- Promotes early literacy.

- Is a form of data collection used regularly by naturalists and scientists. These drawings are useful for later reflection and analysis and as a form of evidence of what children have seen. When used in series, observational drawings provide a record that can help naturalists track changes in living things over time.

2. **TALK ABOUT YOUNG CHILDREN AND REPRESENTATION FOR A FEW MINUTES** (10 minutes). Show overhead 11.2 (a more primitive drawing) and make the following points:

- Three- and four-year-olds are just learning to draw. Their motor abilities are not fully developed and they are just learning about symbolic representation.

- Children's early representations often focus on the overall shape of a plant or animal. Refer to overhead 11.2 as an example. Over time, children's awareness of the parts that make up the whole becomes evident in drawings that represent not just shape, but also different parts. Fine-tip drawing tools are needed to capture these details. Now show overhead 11.3 as a comparison. Note that Alexis has made a fine line to represent the prickles on an aloe plant. Also point out that she has given the plant a face, something young children commonly do.

- Emphasize that children need tools and plenty of time to practice.

- Each child will have their own preference for the medium in which they choose to communicate. In part, this is developmental—can they grasp a big marker or pen? It may also be a difference in style. Some children prefer three-dimensional representation, such as clay or collage, and others prefer movement.

- Mention that movement is an excellent form of representation. It can be used to capture characteristics such as movement of an animal or growth of a plant.

ENCOURAGING REPRESENTATION THROUGH CONVERSATIONS (30 MINUTES)

PURPOSE: Teachers will generate a list of strategies they can use to encourage representation in their own classrooms.

1. **INTRODUCE AND SHOW VIGNETTE 5** (15 minutes). Start by telling your teachers that this vignette was filmed in a Boston Head Start program. It shows a teacher and five children working at a table, drawing small plants. Distribute the vignette observation form and transcript, and ask teachers to note strategies the teacher in the video uses to encourage representation and engage children with science.

Show the vignette and ask teachers what they noticed. Note their strategies on the chart you prepared. Ask how these strategies promote science learning.

Look for ideas like these:

- Provides hand lenses to help children look closely at details
- Calls attention to parts of the plants, using accurate terms
- Listens attentively, responding to their comments and accepting naïve conceptions
- Calls attention to details such as color
- Helps children label their drawings, as a scientist would

2. **INTRODUCE THE SECOND VIEWING** (15 minutes). Ask teachers to think about children's naïve conceptions and ways the teacher might immediately respond and later follow up. Show the vignette. Then ask teachers to think about the worm sequence in particular. Ask, "Do you have any alternate ideas for responding?" Continue to add strategies to the chart.

Look for ideas like these:

- Asking what makes it look like a worm and then if it is different in others ways. In conclusion, the teacher might ask if children still think it is a worm and if not, what they think it is.
- Comparing the worm to another worm (or a picture of a worm). Have the child look at the two together and think about how they are the same and how they are different.

ENCOURAGING REPRESENTATION— THE ENVIRONMENT AND ROUTINES (10 MINUTES)

PURPOSE: An important part of encouraging representation is the choice of materials and their accessibility, as well as regular routines. This conversation will highlight key strategies.

1. **TALK ABOUT THE SELECTION OF MATERIALS FOR A FEW MINUTES** (5 minutes). Ask teachers how the selection of materials can encourage representation. Note their strategies on the chart, seeing that the following points are made:
   - Materials must be selected that allow for accurate representation of the object's characteristics. For example, drawing is a medium that allows for representation of many characteristics but only two dimensions. The amount of detail possible varies with the type of pen or marker being used. Fine-tip markers allow for more detail. Wire is a medium that is excellent for re-creating shape but might not be good for capturing all of the details. Mention that their expectations should be in line with the medium's potential.
   - Various materials should be available. Consider both two- and three-dimensional material as important. While observational drawing is particularly important for naturalists, there are other effective media such as collage and clay or wire sculpture.
   - Adding props for dramatic play (such as field guides, hand lenses, and live plants) encourages children to take on the role of naturalist.

2. **Talk about the importance of accessibility** (2 to 3 minutes). Ask teachers how to display materials so they inspire representation. Be sure to make the following points:

   - Children should be able to get materials and put them back without help.

   - Materials should be available indoors and outdoors.

   - Clipboards are especially useful for outdoor drawing.

   - Representation should be done when the object is in view.

3. **Talk about the importance of regular routines** (5 minutes). Ask teachers how regular routines support children's representation. Note their strategies on the chart and be sure to make the following points:

   - While two-and three-dimensional work can be encouraged when materials are available, opportunities for movement don't come as naturally. Teachers must schedule time in the daily routine.

   - Verbal encouragement or suggestions from teachers is important while children are examining organisms, particularly if they are not making representations. Give a few examples such as, "I see you have noticed the rings on the worms. Do you think you could draw them? (Or make them with clay?)" Or, "Can you show me with your body how the worm moves?"

   - Large group time is a good time to show that you value children's work by sharing it. This is also a good time to offer opportunities for movement.

4. **Finally, talk about displaying children's work** (2 to 3 minutes). Make these points about things teachers should consider as they display children's work:

   - Displaying children's work shows that you value what they do.

   - Displays allow children to revisit their work and build on their ideas.

   - Displays should be at the children's eye level.

   - Displays should reflect children's current interests and investigations.

Help Teachers Assess Children's Representations (30 minutes)

Purpose: This activity will help participants understand how children represent living things. By carefully reflecting on and assessing children's representations, teachers can learn about children's inquiry skills and their science understanding.

1. **Introduce the activity** (5 minutes). Tell teachers that they will be looking at some children's work samples and talking about the science understandings being communicated. Ask the teachers to open the teacher's guide to the outcomes chart in the appendices. Explain that they will refer to this chart as they assess children's work. Distribute the document annotations and refer to their placement in the teacher's guide. Make the following points:

- Note that using the forms will help teachers focus their analysis of each piece of work. These completed forms can also help parents or caregivers appreciate what their children are learning.

- Representations are best understood in conjunction with a conversation where the children elaborate on their own meaning of their work. The following samples were selected to highlight this point.

2. **SHOW AND DISCUSS OVERHEADS** (25 minutes). Show as many overheads (11.5–11.8) as time allows. Ask teachers to talk about what they see and what they might write on a document annotation.

OVERHEAD 11.5: NICK'S TURTLE

Context: Nick is in kindergarten and engaged in nature exploration. His class has a pet turtle.

Science being explored/evidence: Nick has represented many of the physical characteristics of the turtle (including shape, pattern on shell, toes, tail, and head).

Given the smile on the turtle's face, a good discussion topic for the teacher and Nick would be to get him to describe the real turtle's face.

OVERHEAD 11.6: ROBBIE'S SNAIL

Context: Robbie is a young three-year-old who has just arrived in a class that is in the middle of an exploration of nature.

Science being explored/evidence: Robbie has noticed that snails have shells and may have associated it with his own house, but we can't be sure of that. The rest of his dictation is fantasy. While Robbie's capacity for symbolic representation is limited, he is engaged in the exploration.

The teacher might ask Robbie to identify where the shell is and talk about what he noticed. This would heighten Robbie's observation skills.

OVERHEAD 11.7: KENNY'S CRICKET

Context: All we know is that Kenny is a preschooler in a classroom that is exploring plants and animals.

Science being explored/evidence: Kenny has noticed physical and behavioral characteristics of his cricket. He has identified several body parts for the cricket and that petals on the flowers are the food. His depiction of the food shows his understanding of the needs of living things.

A conversation with Kenny might focus on the features he has represented and their relationship to the actual cricket.

OVERHEAD 11.8: MAXIEL'S WORMS

Context: Maxiel is in a Head Start class that is engaged in an exploration of nature.

Science being explored/evidence: This drawing shows the kind of complexity revealed by young children when their representation work is valued and their observations are focused. He drew worms in a variety of ways. The most interesting example shows a worm eating dirt, probably based on an observation he made. It reflects an understanding of the physical characteristics of the worm in a particular circumstance, as well as an understanding of the worm's needs.

A good conversation topic with Maxiel would be to get him talking about what he saw when the worm ate and how he has shown it here.

Show overhead 11.4. Encourage teachers to use this form to annotate photos, work samples, transcripts, or any other documents that they may have. When filling out the form, teachers should highlight children's inquiry skills and their understanding of science concepts. Teachers should attach their annotation to each document.

Close by letting the teachers know about the next professional development activity, as well as the time and location.

Suggested next steps

- Make a handout of the strategies and distribute it.

- Follow up with workshop 12, which builds on the content of this workshop.

- Plan guided discussions in which the teachers can share and discuss representations and useful strategies for encouraging representation.

- Conduct observations, helping teachers develop a repertoire of strategies for encouraging representation in their classrooms.

- Suggest readings from the references:

"A Child Constructs an Understanding of a Water Wheel in Five Media," by George Forman (*Childhood Education*, 1996)

"Negotiating with Art Media to Deepen Learning," by George Forman (*Child Care Information Exchange*, 1996)

Observation Drawing with Children: A Framework for Teachers, by N. R. Smith (Teachers College Press, 1998)

TRANSCRIPT OF VIDEO VIGNETTE 5: ENCOURAGING REPRESENTATION

Scene: Five children are sitting around a table making observational drawings of small plants. The children include Ronald *(green striped jersey)*, Alyiah *(chartreuse jersey)*, and Gabriela *(pink striped jersey)*.

Teacher: Do you want to study plants? To see the different parts of the plants? So I want you to draw the plants. Use the lens to look at it and draw it. *(Passes out paper.)*

(Ronald shows plant to the teacher.)

Teacher: Which part of the root?

Ronald: *(Points to the plant)* This here.

Teacher: That part of the root?

Ronald: *(Takes lens and examines the root)* I see a bug.

Teacher: Oh, you see a bug? *(Teacher looks through lens at root)* What kind of bug?

Ronald: *(Inaudible)* It eats people.

Teacher: *(Pointing to child's drawing)* So, where is the bug on your plant?

Ronald: *(Points to bottom of drawing, then points again to upper part of plant)* This is the "up" part.

Teacher: The "up" part? *(Pulls gently at leaves of plant)* What's up top? What is this? What are these?

Ronald: *(Pulls at leaves)* Leaves. These are leaves. *(Points to drawing.)*

Teacher: So these are the leaves. So what color your leaves are *(inaudible)*.

Ronald: Green.

Teacher: So you want to put green for your leaves. *(Hands Ronald a green marker.)*

Alyiah: Look at mine, Imelda. *(Holds up drawing.)*

Teacher: Okay, you ready to talk about yours? Come over on this side. Bring your plant with you so we can talk about it.

(Video briefly shows another girl, Alyson, looking at plant through lens and drawing on paper.)

(Alyson sits next to the teacher.)

Teacher: Oh, this is interesting. Show me the roots. Where are the roots?

Alyson: Right here. *(Points to drawing.)*

Teacher: You want to write the word "roots"? Write where the roots are.

(The teacher writes word on another piece of paper. The child writes the word "root" near the root on her drawing.)

Teacher: So, what is this area? *(Points to stem on child's drawing.)*

Alyson: That's a worm. *(Points to small line near stem.)*

Teacher: So, that's a worm on your plant? *(Writes the word on another piece of paper)* Okay, write your word. Write it beside your worm.

(Alyson writes word)

Teacher: *(Points to parts on drawing)* So now you have your roots. You have a worm on your plant. Which part of your plant is the worm on?

(The teacher is now sitting with Gabriela.)

Teacher: Do you want to tell me about your picture?

Gabriela: *(Points to drawing)* That's the root and this is the leaves and the *(inaudible)*.

Teacher: *(Points to drawing as she speaks)* Okay, so this is the root. Which part—this is a . . .

Gabriela: The fruit.

Teacher: A fruit? What kind of fruit do you think it is?

Gabriela: Like a potato.

Teacher: Like a potato. Shaped like a potato. So you think it is a potato? *(Points to drawing)* So you said this part of your plant is the fruit part. This part is the . . .

Gabriela: *(Shrugs)*

Teacher: *(Points to stem on drawing)* You don't know what it is? And you said this part is the leaves. Okay, where's the stem?

Gabriela: *(Points to part between fruit and leaves on her drawing)* Stem is right here.

Teacher: So, this is the stem and what does the stem do to the plant? How the water get to the . . . *(Interrupted by another child showing her a drawing.)*

Gabriela: They grow.

Teacher: How the plant grow? How does the plant get water?

Gabriela: With seeds. With water and seeds. You put the seeds and they drink. Then they grow. *(Puts hands up in the air.)*

Teacher: So, what do they do with the seeds?

Gabriela: They can put it in water.

Teacher: They can put it in water. So you can put seed in water? Can it grow in water too?

Gabriela: *(Nods)* And it grows like fruit.

Teacher: So do you want to write the words—leaves, stem . . . ?

Gabriela: Fruit.

(Teacher writes words on another piece of paper.)

Gabriela: *(Inaudible)*

Teacher: How about roots? Look at this. *(Takes plant in hand and shows roots to Gabriela.)*

Gabriela: The root.

Teacher: Okay, so you gonna write the word "leaf" and what you say this one again?

(The teacher continues to write words.)

Gabriela: Fruit.

Teacher: Fruit. And this one is . . .

Gabriela: Stem.

Teacher: Stem. Right. And. . .

Gabriela: This is the leaf. *(Points to word that teacher has written and then points to leaf on her drawing and writes word on drawing)* I did it.

Teacher: Oh, nice. Now the stem.

Gabriela: The stem. *(Points to word.)*

ADVANCED WORKSHOP 5: VIGNETTE OBSERVATION FORM

Note your observations by identifying the teacher strategies and child responses in separate columns.

Child Behavior/Comments	Teacher Response

Using Children's Representations as Teaching Tools

AT A GLANCE

Purpose:

- Examine the ways representation can be used to deepen children's science learning
- Have science talks about children's representations

Activity	Time	Materials
Help teachers assess children's representations Help participants, working in small groups, to assess representations from their own classrooms.	30 minutes	• Document annotations
Discuss using representations as teaching tools Use vignettes to help participants identify strategies for using representations to deepen children's science understandings.	40 minutes	• Chart: "Strategies for Talking About Representations" • VCR, monitor, and video cued to vignette 6: "Talking About Worm Drawing" and vignette 7: "Talking About Plant Drawing" • Overhead projector screen and overheads 11.4 and 12.1 • Copies of vignette observation form and transcripts for vignettes 6 and 7
Help teachers use children's representations to stimulate science talks Support teachers as they plan goals and questions for a conversation with one of their children about their representation.	20 minutes	• Science talk planning form

Pre-assignment: Bring three observational drawings or other forms of representation (such as a collage or a clay sculpture) to the workshop.

Advanced Workshop 12:
Using Children's Representations as Teaching Tools

OBJECTIVES

- Examine ways representation can be used to deepen children's science learning
- Plan science talks about children's representations

OVERVIEW

- Help teachers assess children's representations (30 minutes)
- Discuss using representations as teaching tools (40 minutes)
- Help teachers use children's representations to plan a science talk (20 minutes)

INSTRUCTOR PREPARATION

- **GIVE ASSIGNMENT.** At lest one week before the workshop, ask teachers to collect three to five representations from their class. Suggest diversity, either in children's ability or in the medium used.
- **REVIEW VIGNETTES.** View the vignettes, noting aspects you will highlight in the workshop.

> The activities in this workshop assume that teachers have already participated in advanced workshop 11. In workshop 11, they learn to fill out document annotations, and in this workshop they start using them to assess their own children's work.

MATERIALS

- Chart: "Strategies for Talking About Representation"
- VCR, monitor, and video cued to vignette 6: "Talking About Worm Drawing" and vignette 7: "Talking About Plant Drawing"
- Overhead projector, screen, and overheads 11.4 and 12.1
- Copies of document annotations, transcripts for vignettes 6 and 7, science talk planning form, and vignette observation form for everyone

Activity

HELP TEACHERS ASSESS CHILDREN'S REPRESENTATIONS (30 MINUTES)

PURPOSE: This activity will help teachers apply what they are learning as they assess what children's representation reveal about their science understandings.

1. **INTRODUCE THE WORKSHOP AND FIRST TASK** (5 minutes). Provide an overview of the workshop activities. Then show overhead 11.4—the sample document annotation—and review how to fill one out. Pass out two forms to everyone and ask them to select two of the samples they brought that show distinctly different medium or skill levels. Suggest they refer to the outcomes chart in the resources section of the teacher's guide to complete a document annotation for each of the two samples they have selected. Ask them to form questions on another piece of paper. Tell teachers they have fifteen minutes to complete this task.

2. **SUPPORT TEACHERS AS THEY COMPLETE THE DOCUMENT ANNOTATION FORMS** (20 minutes). Go around the room and check on individuals. Help them think through what they want to write when they seem stuck. As they complete their forms, ask them to partner with another teacher who is done. Their partners might have additional thoughts as they examine children's representations.

3. **ASK TEACHERS TO SHARE THEIR THOUGHTS ABOUT THIS EXPERIENCE** (5 minutes). Listen to comments and provide support as teachers think through issues. Teachers might say it was easier to assess representation if they had discussions with children about their work. Emphasize how conversations with children can provide added insights into their work, what they are trying to accomplish, and their science understandings.

USING REPRESENTATIONS AS TEACHING TOOLS (30 MINUTES)

PURPOSE: Talking to children about their representations can help teachers assess children's understandings. Such conversations also provide a teaching opportunity, helping children to reflect on their experiences and their ideas. This activity will help teachers develop a list of strategies for their use.

1. **DISCUSS THE VARIED WAYS REPRESENTATIONS CAN SERVE AS TEACHING TOOLS** (10 minutes). Show overhead 12.1. Point out the term *documentation*, which includes photographs, data charts, dictations, and children's representations.

OVERHEAD 12.1: USE REPRESENTATIONS TO DEEPEN LEARNING AND PROMOTE INQUIRY

- **Build ability to communicate observations and ideas**
  As children talk about their work, encourage them to describe what they have represented. Model using descriptive language yourself.

- **Focus on particular science ideas**
  For example, talk about the parts of a worm and how they have been represented. You might examine a worm and the child's representation at the same time. Use a series of representations to talk about how plants grow and develop over time, noting the differences from one drawing to the next.

- **Build a culture of inquiry and collaboration**
  Look at children's work with groups of children. Compare and contrast living things by highlighting the different ways they have been represented. What did you notice? How did you find that out?

- **Connect children's explorations from one day to the next**
  Use their work to call attention to what they were doing a day or two ago. This will help them continue an investigation, moving forward with their inquiry.

> - **Recap what has been learned at key points in an exploration**
>   *Use selections of several children's work to review what they have done and learned before moving on.*
> - **Stimulate discussion in which children synthesize and analyze their work**
>   *Use documents to compare, contrast, and draw conclusions about plants and animals they have been exploring.*

Transition to the next activity by saying that they will get a chance to apply these ideas as they look at two vignettes.

2. **VIEW AND DISCUSS VIGNETTE 6: "TALKING ABOUT WORM DRAWING"** (15 minutes). Introduce the vignette by saying that this is Cindy, a teacher from an earlier vignette, and Daphne. Daphne is drawing worms and they are talking about what she is doing. Distribute the vignette observation form. Tell teachers that as they view the vignette, they should note the strategies being used next to the appropriate box.

   Show the vignette. After viewing, ask teachers to identify strategies (and list on prepared chart) the teacher is using and then talk about other ways this drawing might be used. Every representation does not have a use for each learning goal so you don't need to fill in every box.

During the discussion, emphasize how teachers can use representations to deepen children's science understanding and promote inquiry. Look for ideas like these:

- Build ability to communicate observations and ideas—this was a primary goal of this conversation. Cindy is helping Daphne (a child who speaks Spanish) use and learn words for relative size: longest, smallest, middle-sized.
- Focus on particular science ideas—this conversation is focused on describing characteristics of worms, which could lead to a discussion of living and nonliving when children notice the worm is not moving.

Some other suggestions include the following:

- Showing the drawing to Daphne the next day or later in the week so she remembers her interest in the relative size of worms. Revisiting the drawing might lead Daphne to consider other characteristics: physical (talking about how width might influence the way she draws worms) or behavioral (the way they move and rather than tracing them, following them with a marker).
- Comparing Daphne's representation with other children's work and talking about the characteristics of each, and highlighting the varied perspectives and different features that were observed.

3. **VIEW AND DISCUSS VIGNETTE 7: "TALKING ABOUT PLANT DRAWING"** (15 minutes). Repeat the same process with vignette 7. Introduce this vignette by saying it was filmed in another Boston Head Start classroom. The teacher, Imelda, is talking with Alexis about her two drawings. Guide the teachers to use the vignette 7 column on their vignette observation form as they view the vignette.

   After viewing the vignette, discuss strategies the teacher uses to deepen children's science understanding, and add new strategies to your list.

This vignette is similar to the first one. It uses the representation to draw out the science. Look for ideas like these:

- Build ability to communicate observations and ideas—this was a primary goal of this conversation. Imelda elicits descriptive language as she asks the child to compare the two plants and her drawings of them.

- Focus on particular science ideas—this conversation is focused on describing characteristics of these two plants, particularly the ways they differ.

Other ways the drawings might be used include the following:

- Showing the drawings to Alexis the next day, or later in the week, to remind her of the experience. This reflective conversation might lead to new inquiry, such as looking for other leaf shapes or wondering how the "prickles" help the plant.

- Comparing Alexis's representations with other children's work and talking about the characteristics of each; highlighting the varied perspectives and different features that were observed.

PLANNING A CONVERSATION ABOUT CHILDREN'S REPRESENTATIONS (20 MINUTES)

PURPOSE: This activity will help the teachers apply to their own classroom what they are learning about using representations as teaching tools.

1. **SET UP THIS PLANNING TASK** (5 minutes) by distributing the representation conversation planning form. Tell teachers that you are going to give them a chance to use one of the representations to guide a conversation that furthers children's science learning and promotes inquiry. Review the form and answer any questions they have.

2. **GIVE THEM TEN MINUTES TO WORK.** Wander around the room and help those who seem to be struggling. Encourage teachers to talk to each other as they work.

3. **BRING THEM TOGETHER TO SHARE IDEAS** (5 minutes). Allow a few minutes for a few of them to share ideas and solve any issues that arise. Encourage them to follow through and have this conversation. Make a point of telling teachers that while this workshop is focused on using children's representations, all forms of documentation can be used as teaching tools in this same way. This would include photographs and records of data.

In conclusion, let them know about the next professional development, when and where it takes place, and which assignments they should complete.

Suggested Next Steps

- Make a handout of the strategies list and distribute it.

- You might follow up with a workshop about making documentation panels.

- Conduct guided discussions in which teachers bring documentation (video or audiotape) of conversations about children's representations, and analyze them together.

- Observe and have a conference with teachers around a conversation about representation.

- Suggest reading from the bibliography:

"Negotiating with Art Media to Deepen Learning," by George Forman (*Child Care Information Exchange*, 1996)

Helping Children Ask Good Questions, by George Forman (Exchange Press, 1996)

Transcript of Video Vignette 6:
Talking About Worm Drawing

Scene: Daphne is sitting at a table, next to live worms, drawing with marker drawing.

Teacher: Are you tracing your worms?

Daphne: *(Makes line with marker on paper)* I did it! I did it!

Teacher: Did you trace your worms the same size?

Daphne: Yes. *(Points to paper)* It's too much.

Teacher: It's too much what?

Daphne: *(Points to big worm)* It's too long.

Teacher: That's the longest one, isn't it?

Daphne: This is the real tiny one. *(Points to small worm on paper.)*

Teacher: That's the smallest one.

Daphne: *(Points to worm on paper)* This is big.

Teacher: What about this one? Is that the middle-size one?

Daphne: Yes and this is the baby one. *(Points to small worm)* That's the father. *(Points to larger worm.)*

Teacher: What makes you say that's the father worm?

Daphne: Because he's too bigger.

Teacher: Because he's too big. What else did you notice about the worms?

Daphne: *(Straightens out large worm on paper)* See?

Teacher: You're holding him out straight to see how long he is?

Daphne: Little tiny one is moving too fast. *(Points to paper)* This one is not moving.

Teacher: Wonder why that one's not moving.

TRANSCRIPT OF VIDEO VIGNETTE 7:
TALKING ABOUT PLANT DRAWINGS

Scene: Teacher (Imelda) and Alexis are sitting at a table. Plants are on the table, and two drawings are in front of Alexis.

Imelda: *(Points to large plant)* Look at this plant and look at your plant and talk about it. *(Points back and forth from drawing to plant.)*

Alexis: *(Takes large leaf in her hand)* This one has holes and this one *(points to drawing)* has not.

Imelda: So, this one has holes. Where are the holes?

Alexis: *(Takes leaf and points to ridges on leaf.)*

Imelda: Oh, so those are the holes? So this part here *(points to leaves on drawing, then to plant leaf)* is this part right here?

Alexis: *(Takes leaf) (inaudible)* plant up. *(Points to drawing)* This one's just down.

Imelda: So, look at the leaf. *(Holds leaf in hand)* Show me the prickles. I see we have prickles. Show me where the prickles are on your leaf.

Alexis: *(Outlines leaf on drawing with her hand.)*

Imelda: What shape is this? The plant.

Alexis: *(Pulls at leaf)* A rectangle.

Imelda: *(Touching leaf)* A rectangle. Can you feel the inside of the leaf? Can you tell me what it feels like?

Alexis: *(Touching leaf)* It feels soft and warm.

Imelda: Soft and warm . . . and the edge of the plant . . .

Alexis: *(Runs hand along edge of leaf)* Rough.

Imelda: It's rough? *(Runs hands on inside of leaf)* And in here it's smooth.

Alexis: *(Touches leaf again) (inaudible)*

Imelda: *(Points to child's other drawing)* Now this one over here. Look at this one. *(Points to other plant and also first plant)* Now tell me the difference between this plant and this plant.

Alexis: *(Points to first plant)* This one is *(inaudible)* and this one *(points to second plant)* is *(inaudible)* because this one look like a heart and this one *(points to second drawing)* looks like a heart.

Imelda: So this looks like a heart and what this one look like? *(Points to first plant.)*

Alexis: A rectangle.

Imelda: A rectangle.

Alexis: They're both shapes.

Imelda: So, they're both shapes. What is [it] you want to tell me. They're both shapes. One is rectangular and one is a heart. What else [do] you want to tell me about it?

ADVANCED WORKSHOP 12: VIGNETTE OBSERVATION FORM

Note your observations by identifying the teacher strategies and child responses in separate columns.

Goal of Strategy	Strategies in Vignette 6	Strategies in Vignette 7
Build capacity to communicate observations and ideas		
Focus on particular science ideas		
Build a culture of inquiry and collaboration		
Connect children's explorations from one day to the next		
Recap what has been learned		
Help children synthesize and analyze their work		

ADVANCED WORKSHOP 12:
REPRESENTATION CONVERSATION PLANNING FORM

Name: _____

Child: _____

Goal(s) of conversation: _____

_____

_____

Science content to explore : _____

List a few questions that you can use to get the conversation going, and search for deeper meanings along the way. Note the part of the representation that each question might be focused on—for example, you might want to talk about the color used for a worm or the shape of a leaf or petal.

Facilitating Science Talks

AT A GLANCE

Purpose:

- Build an understanding of group conversations and the role they play in children's science learning
- Build various strategies for facilitating science talks
- Build an awareness of what inhibits conversations

Activity	Time	Materials
Provide an overview of science talks Let teachers share their early attempts at science talks, the successes and issues. Begin to talk about effective and ineffective strategies.	30 minutes	• Charts: "Strategies for Science Talks" and "Issues We Are Having with Science Talks" • Overhead projector, screen, and overheads 13.1–13.3
Help teachers analyze a small group science talk Use a vignette to highlight the importance of science talks and identify strategies teachers can use to facilitate them.	30 minutes	• VCR, monitor, and video cued to vignette 8: "Snail Science Talk" • Copies of handouts: vignette observation form and transcript of vignette 8
Help teachers analyze a large group science talk Use a transcript to highlight the importance of large group science talks and identify strategies teachers can use to facilitate them.	30 minutes	• Copies of "Strategies for Facilitating Science Talks" and "Transcript Analysis Form"

Pre-assignment: Participants will be asked to pay attention as they talk with children, noting where they are successfully engaging them in thinking about science and where they are having difficulty. They should also complete the "Read and Reflect" assignment.

Advanced Workshop 13: Facilitating Science Talks

OBJECTIVES

- Build an understanding of group conversations and the role they play in children's science learning
- Build various strategies for facilitating science talks
- Build an awareness of what inhibits conversations

OVERVIEW

- Provide overview of science talks (30 minutes)
- Help teachers analyze a small group science talk (30 minutes)
- Help teachers analyze a large group science talk (30 minutes)

INSTRUCTOR PREPARATION

- **GIVE ASSIGNMENT.** At least one week before the workshop, distribute the "Read and Reflect" assignment. Also ask teachers to pay attention as they talk with children, noting when they are succeeding and where they have difficulty.
- **REVIEW VIGNETTE.** View the vignette, noting the aspects you will highlight during the workshop.

MATERIALS

- Video vignette 8: "Snail Science Talk," VCR, and monitor
- Copies of handouts: vignette observation form, transcript of vignette 8, "Read and Reflect" assignment, and "Strategies for Facilitating Science Talks"
- Charts: "Strategies for Science Talks" and "Issues We Are Having with Science Talks"
- Overhead projector, screen, and overheads 13.1–13.3

Activity

OVERVIEW OF SCIENCE TALKS (30 MINUTES)

PURPOSE: This activity will set the stage for analyzing science conversations with young children. It will allow participants to share their successes and issues, expand their repertoire of strategies, and begin to overcome barriers they may be experiencing.

1. **INTRODUCE THE WORKSHOP** and begin to identify strategies for promoting conversations with naturalists (15 minutes).

a. Remind teachers of the importance of conversations in building children's understandings. Review these points:

- Conversation stimulates and makes explicit the thinking processes that underlie several aspects of inquiry (collecting data, synthesizing and analyzing data, and using language to communicate). It is also an essential aspect of collaboration.

- Sharing ideas stimulates scientific activity among peers.

- Children's experiences and ideas are more easily recorded for future reference when they put words to their actions.

- In addition to the ways they benefit science learning, conversations build language capacity and promote early literacy.

b. For a few minutes, allow teachers to share successful strategies for facilitating science talks, as well as issues they have encountered. Use the posters you have made to record their comments and ideas. As they share, ask some questions: "Why do you say that strategy worked? What is the evidence of its success? How did it promote science inquiry and learning? How did the children respond?" Try to address the issues during the workshop.

2. **PROVIDE A FRAMEWORK** for further discussion of conversations (15 minutes) using overheads 13.1–13.3. Start with important aspects of conversations that are science focused. Then introduce the idea that there are strategies to avoid. Finally introduce the settings in which science conversations can occur.

OVERHEAD 13.1: FOCUS ON SCIENCE CONCEPTS BY PROMOTING INQUIRY

- **Responses that promote reflection**

    – *Restate or paraphrase a child's statement.*

    – *Ask children for their ideas, such as what makes something alive or how an animal moves or eats.*

    – *Accept their ideas without judgment.*

    Teachers can encourage children's reflection by listening carefully and restating without judgment. Teachers can also communicate that they value children's ideas by giving nonverbal cues such as head nods and verbal acknowledgments such as, "That's an interesting idea."

- **Responses that promote analysis**

    – *Ask for descriptive details*

    – *Ask for examples, comparisons, and alternatives*

    – *Ask, "What if . . . ? Why do you think so? How do you know?"*

    Describing their observations sets the stage for analysis. When teachers ask why or how, they are looking for the evidence that underlies children's ideas.

Overhead 13.2: Responses that Inhibit or Limit Thinking

- **Responses that inhibit children's thinking**

  - *Explaining the phenomenon to the children*

  - *Cutting children off*

  - *Correcting or telling children what to think*

  These are all common responses that teachers have been using for years. They will need to listen to themselves and work to replace these responses with some that encourage thinking.

- **Responses that limit children's thinking**

  - *Lead them to the "correct" answer*

  - *Tell them what to do*

  - *Move on too quickly*

  Teachers often respond using the "strategies" above, particularly the last one. It takes time to think, and we need to give children time before probing for further responses.

Overhead 13.3: Settings for Science Conversations

- **Talks with small groups**
  This is an especially important strategy because small group science talks can involve everyone. This setting can be used to reflect on an exploration, what was learned and what it might mean, or to encourage collaborative problem solving and learning from others.

- **Talks with the whole group**
  Whole group science talks help children learn from others. Hearing what others have seen and done can help children reflect on their observations, while focusing their attention on the characteristics and needs of living things. Data from multiple experiences can come together and support the analysis process. Various theories will come forward for comparison. At the same time, these science talks can give children ideas for how they can engage in future explorations, while engaging reluctant naturalists.

- **Talks with materials or documents at the center**
  With both large and small groups, it is important to bring the concrete into the setting. Plants, animals, photographs, representations, records of data all help children connect with their investigations.

Talking with Small Groups (30 minutes)

Purpose: This activity will help participants focus on the role of conversations in deepening children's thinking.

Reinforce ideas by viewing and discussing a small group science talk. Introduce vignette 8 by saying that it was taped in a Head Start classroom in Boston. It features a lunch table discussion where children share their ideas about how snails move. All of the children in this conversation are English language learners. (See suggestions below to talk about the strategies used to support the engagement of these children.) Give each teacher the vignette observation form for note taking and the transcript.

After viewing the vignette, ask for teachers' observations, "How did this teacher use the talk to engage the children with inquiry and the science concepts?" Ask for specific examples of strategies and why she may have used them by asking, "What exactly did she say? Why do you think she did that?" Or, "What did that strategy provide for the children?"

Highlight the following points when discussing the vignette:

- Teacher engages children in inquiry (you might want to refer to the inquiry diagram here), helping them to communicate their observations and draw conclusions about how snails move. The teacher then uses the conversation to collect data, which she will use later to further the inquiry.

- Teacher engages children with the science concepts, focusing them on the characteristics (movement behavior) of snails.

- Teacher's strategies: The teacher articulates key questions, encourages children to communicate their ideas, and rephrases what children have said to help them respond to or build upon each other's ideas. Note: The teacher does not provide "correct" answers; rather, she accepts all ideas, while encouraging children to share their observations and their different ideas. She uses children's names to bring them into the conversation and acknowledge their contributions.

- Some teachers might suggest that this teacher talks a lot, which can be an excellent point of discussion.

- Ask participants to focus on the teacher's goal—to deepen children's inquiry and understanding about how snails move—and to comment on the role her talk has in meeting the goal. Invite them to discuss other approaches that might also help meet this goal.

When discussing the English language learners, highlight these strategies:

- Use body language to illustrate ideas being expressed

- Restate with corrections—snail and tail (she corrects "foots" later)

- Build on each other's comments

- Insert descriptive language—slipping, sticky, slimy, crawling

- Draw children back in by referring to their previous contributions, as the teacher does with Christina

LARGE GROUP SCIENCE TALK (30 MINUTES)

PURPOSE: This is an opportunity to observe a teacher who searches for clarification and additional information. She models a strategy that is hard for many teachers to learn on their own.

Facilitate analysis of "Read and Reflect" transcript of a large group science talk. Ask teachers to take out their "Read and Reflect" assignment, reminding them of the conversation from the Ohio kindergarten that they read. Ask them to share ideas in groups of four for the next fifteen minutes. Ask groups to form quickly, and give each group a transcript analysis form. Ask them to record their main ideas on this form for sharing with the large group.

Move around the room, checking that each group is on task and recording their ideas. Bring all groups together to share ideas, following the form. Ask them not to repeat things already listed, adding only new items. Be sure they suggest ways to bring varied data out and encourage diverse ideas. Pay attention to the challenges they list and strategies they suggest. Large group science talks are important, generating enthusiasm and involving children in the work of the more advanced children. They will be most successful if they are not too long and if teachers find ways to engage many children at once. The use of documents helps to illustrate what is being said.

Highlight the following ideas:

- Teacher engages children in inquiry, as they reflect on their observations, sharing their data. Notice how the teacher seeks clarification and additional information.

- Teacher engages children with the science concepts, helping children focus on specific characteristics of the centipede and slug. From the teachers comments, it sounds like their investigation of the slug included watching it move over different kinds of paper.

- Teacher's strategies: The teacher asks probing and clarifying questions, encouraging children to become clearer in the way they share their observations. She shares her own observations, serving as a model for the children.

To conclude, pass out the strategies handout and let teachers know about the next professional development activities, and give them any assignment you want them to do.

Suggested Next Steps

Conducting science talks is a difficult skill for teachers to learn. It will be helpful if you can give them more support as they incorporate science talks into their practice.

- Both workshops on representation have examples of conversations with children that would help teachers build their skills in this area.

- Guided discussions are an excellent way to deepen teacher understanding of science talks. During these discussions, teachers can share video or audio tape conversations from their classrooms and discuss them. Transcribing is time consuming, but a very effective form of documentation for these kinds of conversations.

- Mentoring is another excellent way to support teachers. Observe a conversation, document it, and then talk with the teacher about what she did, reinforcing the strategies she is using and brainstorming ideas for the missed opportunities

TRANSCRIPT OF VIDEO VIGNETTE 8:
SNAIL SCIENCE TALK

Scene: A teacher and six children are sitting around a table eating lunch.

Teacher: You know what I was wondering? I've never held a snail before. When the snail crawls on your arm, what does that feel like?

Child: Tickles.

Teacher: Does it feel sticky and slimy?

Child: Yes.

Teacher: Like slippery? If something was crawling up me and it felt like that, then I would think it didn't feel good.

Child: I think it would.

Teacher: You think it would feel good? Remember we were reading about snails a long time ago and it said they had one big foot? But it doesn't walk with its foot the way we walk. How is it moving? I'm wondering about how it's moving on your arm.

Child: With its slime. He's pushing his body.

Teacher: He's pushing his body with his slime?

Child: With his tail. *(Points to rear.)*

Teacher: What is he doing with his tail do you think?

Child: To move.

Teacher: Christina thinks he's pushing himself with his tail and Anna said he's moving himself with slime. Where do you think the slime comes from?

Child: From the "down" part.

Teacher: You mean from the bottom of his body, Hannah?

Child: Yah!

Teacher: *(Inaudible)*, what do you think about the way the snail moves?

Child: Maybe he's pushing himself with his body.

Teacher: With his body? Maybe he's slipping on your arm when he's walking with his foot. Theresa, what do you think?

Child: He has a whole bunch of foots.

Teacher: *(Inaudible)* thinks he has a whole bunch of foots. I need to write this down about how the snail moves because that's something we're going to be talking about.

Child: *(Speaks, but not that audibly.)*

Teacher: Now you're saying he has a bunch of feet and when he goes, he puts his feet up, and before you said that he's making slime from the bottom part of his body and that makes him move.

Child: He makes back flips.

Teacher: *(Inaudible)* said maybe he's moving his whole body, kind of like the way we move with our muscles? Like when I move my arm and I use muscles?

Child: He moves slowly like this. *(Uses fingers to demonstrate.)*

Teacher: Christina said maybe he's moving his tail to push his body.

Advanced Workshop 13: Transcript Analysis Form

Come to a group agreement about the answers to these questions and note your thoughts on this form. Make specific reference to places in the transcript as you note your responses to the following questions.

1. What aspects of inquiry are these children engaged in? Refer to the inquiry diagram or the outcomes chart as you think about your response.

2. What science concepts are being explored? Again, refer to the outcomes chart as you respond.

3. What strategies is the teacher using to deepen science understanding? Note which strategies seem particularly effective and those that you would like to practice using.

4. What challenges might you have using these strategies in a large group science talk? For each challenge, note a way you might overcome the challenge.

STRATEGIES FOR FACILITATING SCIENCE TALKS

1. Start slowly. For example, you might begin with five- to ten-minute conversations and increase the time as children increase their engagement. Take cues from the children to decide when to stop and when to continue.

2. Choose a concrete stimulus for the conversation. For example, you might choose an actual plant or animal, a child's drawing or photograph of a plant or animal, or a picture from a book.

3. Be enthusiastic and curious. For example, "I am so excited about what happened this morning. Who wants to talk about the plants or animals they observed?"

4. Model ways of sharing your thoughts and some of the questions you have. For example, "Your group said that it took four of you to put your arms around the tree trunk. Why do you think the trunk is so big? I wonder what would happen to the tree if the trunk were really small or soft?"

5. Expand on children's observations and ideas. For example, if Kabir says, "I found a worm," you might rephrase by saying, "Kabir found a worm squiggling around under the leaves."

6. Ask questions to engage children in analysis. For example, "What do you think the ant needs to live? Why do you think so? What do you think we could do to find out?"

7. Ask questions to help children predict. For example, before you go on an outdoor exploration, ask, "What living things do you think we'll find outside today? Where do you think we'll find them?" Be sure to follow by asking why they think so or by getting them to compare different responses.

8. Provide children with the support they need to share their thoughts with the following:
   - Give children time to think before you expect them to respond. Silent time is okay.
   - Find ways for children with limited language and second language learners to demonstrate what they know.
   - Model using descriptive language by explaining a child's actions. For example, "Shannon is showing us how a worm moves. Look at the way she lifts the middle of her body and then stretches forward."

9. Draw out ideas. For example, "Tuan described the ant he saw. Who else saw an ant? What did you see? Did yours also have . . . ?"

10. Avoid comments that inhibit or limit thinking. Avoid the following:
   - Explaining the science phenomena yourself
   - Correcting children
   - Leading them to the "correct" answer
   - Moving on too quickly

READ AND REFLECT 13

Pay attention to the science interactions you have with children. Note the successful strategies you are using for engaging children and getting them to share observations and ideas. Note the difficulties you are having too. Be sure to provide quotes from your conversations to illustrate successes and difficulties.

Successful strategies:

Difficulties:

Read the following transcript from an Ohio kindergarten class and answer the reflection questions.

LARGE GROUP SCIENCE TALK ABOUT CENTIPEDES AND SLUGS

Scene: The whole kindergarten class is gathered on the rug. Children are taking turns sharing their observations of centipedes and slugs.

Scene 1: Centipede Sharing

Teacher: Christopher, could you see the centipede eating grass?

Christopher: *(Holding up a large paper)* Yes.

Teacher: Can you demonstrate how he was eating it? I'm not sure I've seen that before.

Christopher: There's this little thing. I don't know what you call it and that's how the centipede eats.

Teacher: I don't know what you mean by "thing." You need to be a little bit more explicit. That means you need to explain it a little bit like what did it look like. Where was it located? On the critter?

Christopher: It was on the bottom of his face.

Teacher: It was on the bottom of his face. Now, how could you see it so closely?

Christopher: Because when I put him down, he was still backwards and I bent over *(he bends over)* and looked closely *(voice trails off)*.

Teacher: You looked with your eyes and you weren't using a magnifying glass at all?

Christopher: I used that little big thing, you know.

Teacher: The large magnifying glass? This one?

Christopher: Yes.

Teacher: Okay. This is the really large magnifying glass. Tell me exactly how you did that. How did you get your centipede out of the container? How did you get it under this magnifying glass and the, what, specifically, did you see?

Christopher: I took him out with my hands very gently and put him on the paper *(he demonstrates how he did it)* and I turned him over to see anywhere he ate. Then I saw a little teeny hole and I thought it was where he ate. So I put the magnifying glass over *(voice trails off)*.

Teacher: Oh, so when you say you turned him over, you mean it was on the side where the legs were that you saw the little hole.

Christopher: No. It was on the bottom of his face *(points to face)*.

Teacher: On the bottom of his face, you saw a little hole and that's where he was eating. Okay. Christopher, was your face near his leg? How could you tell which part of the critter was his face?

Christopher: Because I saw the antenna. *(Takes both arms and extends out from his head.)*

Scene 2: Slug Sharing

Teacher: It didn't have a hole for something to come out of it.

Boy: No, not even the hole.

Teacher: Okay. Tell me again because I'm not sure I'm understanding.

Boy: I saw some sparkles behind it. *(Waves hand back and forth.)*

Teacher: What did those sparkles look like? Like glitter?

Boy: It looks like glitter.

Teacher: It was sparkling? Where was that coming from?

Boy: *(Shrugs)* I don't know.

Teacher: Anyone else who had a slug know what he's describing?

Girl: *(Inaudible)*

Teacher: Speak up a little louder.

Girl: He's leaving stuff behind.

Teacher: He's leaving stuff behind.

Girl: *(Inaudible)*

Teacher: So, when he walks, you said he's leaving like a trail behind him. Did you see the same kind of trail with your earthworm?

Girl: No.

Teacher: I wonder why. Why in the world is there a trail behind that slug, but there's no trail behind the earthworm.

Child: I thought it was a worm because it didn't have any eyes sticking out.

Teacher: Who has a comment about that? I wonder why there is something being left behind the slug, but we didn't see anything being left behind by the earthworm? Because I was watching, too, when they were showing it to me. I was looking and could very clearly see that trail. If the slug went that way, there was a path right behind it—a trail. So, when I started looking at the earthworms, I said, "Well, maybe there's a trail too." So I watched them and they moved across the paper. I saw them on the colored paper. I saw them on the glossy paper. I saw them on the other paper, which was the newsprint. And I didn't see a trail from the earthworms, but I saw a trail from the slug.

Reflection Questions

1. What aspects of inquiry are these children using? Refer to the inquiry diagram or outcomes as you respond.

2. What science concepts are being explored? Refer to the outcomes chart.

3. What strategies to deepen children's science understanding are being used by the teacher ? Note which strategies seem particularly effective and those that you would like to practice using.

4. What challenges might you have using these strategies in a large group science talk? For each challenge, note a way you might overcome the challenge.

Making and Using Documentation Panels

AT A GLANCE

Purpose:

- Learn about the role documentation panels play in science explorations
- Learn to make and evaluate panels
- Learn to use panels to help children revisit, reflect on, and extend their work

Activity	Time	Materials
Introduce documentation panels Present an overview of the "what" and "why" of documentation panels. Guide teachers as they examine a sample panel.	30 minutes	• Overhead projector, screen, and overheads 14.1–14.5
Help teachers make documentation panels Support teachers as they use documents they have brought from their classrooms to make panels that illustrate a recent science exploration. Ask them to use the criteria to evaluate their own panels and share their learning.	1 hour	• Overhead projector, screen, and overhead 14.6 • Poster-making supplies • Copies of documentation panel feedback form

Pre-assignment: Read "Guidelines for Creating Documentation Panels" in the teacher's guide (p. 142). Complete workshop 14 assignment.

Advanced Workshop 14:
Making and Using Documentation Panels

OBJECTIVES

- Learn about the role documentation panels have in science explorations
- Learn to make and evaluate panels
- Learn to use panels to help children revisit, reflect on, and extend their work

OVERVIEW

- Introduce documentation panels (30 minutes)
- Help teachers make documentation panels (1 hour)

INSTRUCTOR PREPARATION

- **DISTRIBUTE ASSIGNMENT.** At least a week before the workshop, give teachers the workshop 14 assignment. Also tell teachers to read the guidelines for creating documentation panels in the teacher's guide.

MATERIALS

- Overhead projector, screen, and overheads 14.1–14.6
- Poster-making supplies including oak tag, rubber cement, markers, assorted colored paper, scissors
- Copies of handouts: documentation panel feedback form, workshop 14 assignment

Activity

INTRODUCTION TO DOCUMENTATION PANELS (30 MINUTES)

PURPOSE: This discussion provides the essential information about panels—what are they, why they are important, and how to use them.

1. **INTRODUCE THE WORKSHOP** (5 minutes) by telling teachers they will be focusing on a practical skill for the next hour and a half—making documentation panels. At the same time, teachers will see how this process triggers valuable ideas about their work. Confirm that everyone has brought documents for making panels. Pair anyone who did not bring documents with someone who did.

2. **PROVIDE AN OVERVIEW OF THE VALUE OF PANELS** (20 minutes). Connect panels to science learning by showing and discussing the following sequence:

   a. Remind participants of the science goals by reviewing overheads 1.2 and 1.3 and by referring them to the outcomes in the teacher's guide on p. 147. Tell teachers that the main goal of documentation panels is to make the science learning visible. Highlighting children's engagement with science processes and ideas is key.

b. Ask participants to form groups of three. Give each group a copy of overhead 14.1 (a documentation panel). Show overhead 14.2, and review the questions they will use to guide their discussion. Leave the overhead up while they talk.

OVERHEAD 14.2: DOCUMENTATION PANEL DISCUSSION QUESTIONS

- **What is the intended message in this panel? What is the teacher trying to communicate?**
  Look for ideas such as the teacher wanted to show the children's process of inquiry and the learning that came from it.

- **Where is the science engagement and learning in this panel?**
  Look for ideas such as careful observation and the ability to describe characteristics and behaviors, experimentation with stick and cup, and use of tools, such as the magnifying glass and stick (for measurement).

- **How well are these messages communicated? Where is the evidence of children's science learning?**
  Look for ideas such as the use of photos and captions to convey the inquiry process and reflect children's science ideas.

- **How would you change this panel?**
  There might be a reference to the period of time represented on the panel. Some of the pictures might have been taken closer to the action. Teachers may have other ideas too. The question will help them think analytically and identify new approaches.

---

c. After ten minutes, show overhead 14.1 and discuss teachers' responses to each question.

If you have time, show overhead 14.3. Tell participants that while the previous documentation panel focused on a group of children's observations of a worm, this focuses on the ideas and work of an individual child.

You may want to read aloud the teacher's commentary that appears at the bottom of the documentation panel:

Ali's first drawing focused on the shape of the snail shell, which he represented using concentric circles. In his second drawing, he added a head with eyes and a mouth, and began to draw a spiral inside the outer circle. The third drawing shows more of the snail's body and a more complex combination of spirals and circles. In the final drawing Ali includes all these elements. The features are also more well-defined and include tentacles, and there is more attention to the snail's actual colors.

Use the questions on overhead 14.2 to discuss participants' reactions.

Look for ideas like these:

- What is the intended message in this panel?
  Ali has learned a lot about snail's characteristics over time. His drawings show an increasing awareness of the details of the snail's body parts. In his final drawing he gives the snail a smiling face. Such facial features are common in young children's work.

- Where is the science engagement and learning in this panel?
  The photo shows Ali observing, and the drawings reflect his interest in representing what he sees. The teacher's comments at the bottom describe the drawings.

- How well are these messages communicated?
  Drawings, photos, and commentary are clear and support each other.

- Is there any way that you would change this panel?
  Give teachers a chance to share some ideas they have.

3. **ASK TEACHERS HOW THEY WOULD DESCRIBE A DOCUMENTATION PANEL** (5 minutes). You might ask: "How might we define *documentation panel?*" Discuss a few ideas, then show and review overhead 14.4.

OVERHEAD 14.4: WHAT IS A SCIENCE-FOCUSED DOCUMENTATION PANEL?

- **A poster that illustrates science inquiry and learning**
  Share that the real benefit of documentation panels is that they make the process of inquiry and learning visible to teachers, children, and families.

- **A multimedia presentation**
  Explain that a combination of text, photos, and work samples can capture the complexity of the process in which children are engaged. As teachers learn to create panels they will also learn to evaluate the quality of each document they use—which photos actually illustrate engagement and science learning, which representations reveal science understandings, and which quotes from the children communicate important science ideas. Over time, teachers' understanding of science and children's learning deepen as they repeatedly engage in this process.

- **A story that can either take place over time or at one point in time**
  Mention that documentation panels can illustrate one activity or a sequence of activities. Panels that have a narrow focus are more useful in working with children, but panels that span a longer period of time can help teachers evaluate their teaching. Then, they can look for connections from one activity to the next.

---

4. **REVIEW THE USES OF DOCUMENTATION PANELS** (5 minutes) by asking teachers how they might use them. After listening to their ideas for a few minutes, show overhead 14.5.

OVERHEAD 14.5: USES OF DOCUMENTATION PANELS

- **A stimulus for science talks**
  The documentation panel helps children share what they have done with others. It can also be posted in the room for all of the children to refer to as they move forward in their exploration.

- **An opportunity to promote literacy as well as science**
  Children are eager to "read" their own stories and will learn a lot from the process of "reading" panels.

- **Educate families**
  Panels on display provide families with insights into what children are doing and the science they are learning. Keep families and your colleagues in mind as potential audiences for documentation panels.

- **Teacher reflection**
  The process of making the panel is a valuable opportunity for teachers to reflect on their work and consider next steps to take with these children and the whole group.

MAKING DOCUMENTATION PANELS (1 HOUR)

PURPOSE: This activity allows participants to reflect on the science teaching and learning in their classroom as they learn to create a panel that they can use with children and families.

1. **INTRODUCE THE ACTIVITY** (10 minutes) by telling teachers that they will now have a chance to make a panel. Show overhead 14.6 as a review.

OVERHEAD 14.6: MAKING DOCUMENTATION PANELS

- **Identify a science exploration focus to illustrate**
  Keep science concept(s) and inquiry skill(s) at the forefront of your message. You might focus on a discovery children have made, something they found on an exploration, data collected, or ideas generated by comparing two sets of data (such as facts about a snail and a worm), to name a few.

- **Collect documents that will help tell stories**
  Collect work samples, photographs, dialogue, and observational notes that tell the story.

- **Arrange documents on posterboard**
  Arrange documents left to right and in chronological order. When you are satisfied with the arrangement, glue them down and add captions.

- **Add a title that focuses on your readers**
  Be sure your title communicates your key message.

Review the available materials (oak tag, rubber cement, markers, and so on). Tell teachers that their task is to organize a presentation of the documents they have brought. Remind them to add captions that explain what is shown in the photos and work samples.

Suggest they open their teacher's guides to the science outcomes chart. Tell teachers that they can use this chart to highlight how children used the inquiry skills or explored different science concepts.

> **Instructors Notes**
>
> Watch out! Creating documentation panels is sometimes considered an appropriate place for teacher decorations. You may need to remind some that this is about science learning and that decorations can detract from the important message about the children's engagement and learning.

Allow twenty-five minutes to lay out panels.

2. **SUPPORT THEIR WORK** (25 minutes) by wandering around the room. Answer questions and listen to their discussion to be sure they are on track and moving ahead.

3. **ASK THEM TO USE THE CRITERIA** (15 minutes) on the documentation panel feedback form to evaluate their own panel. Pass out the forms and let teachers know that they can continue to work on their panel. However, while they are working, they should consider how well their panel meets the criteria. Join in these discussions as you move around the room, sharing your own thoughts. Let them know when you will bring them together. It is not essential that they finish their panels—they can always do it after the workshop. If some finish early, encourage them to wander around and look at what others have done.

4. **BRING THEM TOGETHER FOR FINAL COMMENTS** after ten minutes. Ask a few groups to comment on particular decisions they made that highlight the process and the different approaches they have taken. You might want to ask what they learned from considering the criteria and what they would do differently next time. Other possible discussion questions might include the following:

   - Which inquiry skill(s) did you decide to focus on? Why? How did you decide on the concept?

   - While making your panel, what have you learned about science teaching and learning? Keep teachers focused on their own panel and what they might have learned about the children or their own teaching as they reflected on the documents.

   - What did you learn by looking at other panels? Again, keep the focus on children's engagement and learning and on the teacher's role. If teachers have obviously benefited by sharing their work, encourage them to think about how they can continue to do this. Suggest that in addition to sharing panels, they can also share and discuss photographs, children's work samples, or audiotaped conversations.

   - How might you use this panel with your children? Ask, "What do you hope the children will gain?" Look for ideas such as, "I would take the panel to a science talk to help children share what they did with the others, and I would post it in the room so others can refer to it." Such activities can stimulate children's thinking and help them revisit and build on their ideas and experiences, as well as those of others.

In closing, encourage teachers to share their panels and to use them with children and families. Remind them when and where the next workshop or study group is and what they need to do to prepare.

Suggested Next Steps

- Follow up with teachers, asking how they are using panels in their classrooms. Have they displayed them at child's eye level? Did they use them to encourage a science talk? How did it go?

- Offer a workshop on science talks or using children's representations as teaching tools, which will give teachers ideas about how to use the panels to stimulate conversations.

- Focus a few guided discussions on the use of panels with children, allowing teachers to share and analyze their experiences.

- Offer to help teachers who are interested in forming a documentation panel group. Supply a space, supplies, and tools for them to use when they get together to make panels.

DOCUMENTATION PANEL FEEDBACK FORM

Name: _____

Panel: _____

Use the following criteria as you consider the panel's effectiveness:

- Is the science content, with which the children were engaged, evident? What is it? Where is the evidence?

- Is children's inquiry process evident? What is it? Where is the evidence?

- Does the panel provide important background information? Do you understand what you need to know about the setting, timing, and what the children were doing?

- How well do photographs capture children's engagement and actions?

- How well do the work samples and quotes illustrate the important message about science engagement and learning?

- One thing that is really good about this panel:

- One suggestion for improvement:

ADVANCED WORKSHOP 14 ASSIGNMENT

1. Read the section about documentation panels on p. 142 in the teacher's guide. Review the curriculum and look for places where the directions ask you to make a documentation panel.

2. Identify an aspect of your children's exploration that you would like to document.

3. Collect a set of three or four documents that you can use to create a panel that reflects your children's engagement in science inquiry. Use the following guidelines when collecting:
   - Documents should all be related to a particular aspect of your exploration. For example, they might be from an investigation of leaves or a study of the ways that worms move.
   - The document should be varied, including some or all of the following: children's drawings or paintings, photos of three-dimensional representations, photos of children engaged in the exploration, quotes from their conversation, predictions, and conclusions.

The Culture of Inquiry

- A respect for living things

- An emphasis on inquiry

- Sharing observations and ideas

- Recording observations and experiences

- A focus on actual living things

The Science Teacher's Goals

- Encourage children's discovery of the natural world

- Guide children's inquiry

- Deepen children's science understanding

SCIENCE TEACHING AND LEARNING

- Young children develop ideas about science from their life experiences

- New experiences lead children to challenge previous naïve ideas

- A balance between exploration and thinking, reasoning, and theorizing provides a strong basis for learning

- Inquiry that leads to science learning takes time

- When guided, children have the ability to engage in all aspects of the inquiry process

Key Ideas about this Approach to Science Learning

- Building understanding of important science concepts is an appropriate goal for young children.

- Children naturally form ideas about the world based on their life experiences.

- In inquiry-based science our role is to provide new experiences that can lead children to more sophisticated theories.

"Experience is not the best teacher.
It sounds like heresy, but when you think about it, it's
reflection on experience that makes it educational."

—George Forman,
Professor Emeritus, University of Massachusetts

Key Elements of Discovering Nature with Young Children Assessment Process

- Collecting data

- Analyzing data regularly

- Drawing conclusions and making decisions

SHERRI'S PLANT

NOAH'S PLANT

ALEXIS'S PLANT

SAMPLE DOCUMENT ANNOTATION

DOCUMENT ANNOTATION

Child(ren): _____

Context/Setting: _____

Date: _____

_____

Science Concepts Explored/Evidence: _____

_____

_____

_____

NICK'S TURTLE

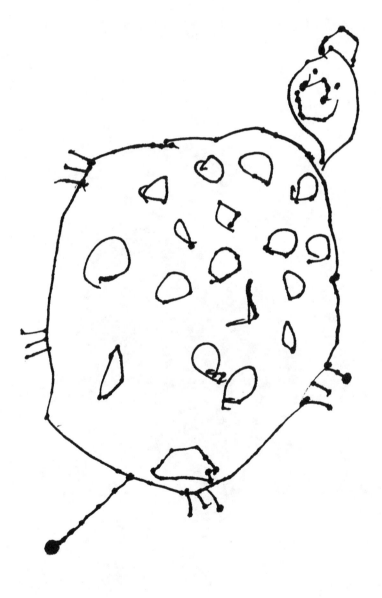

Robbie's Snail

Kenny's Cricket

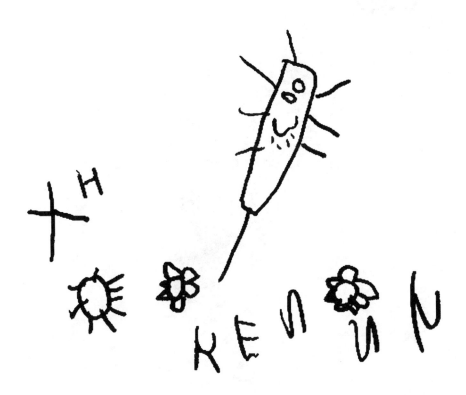

MAXIEL'S WORMS

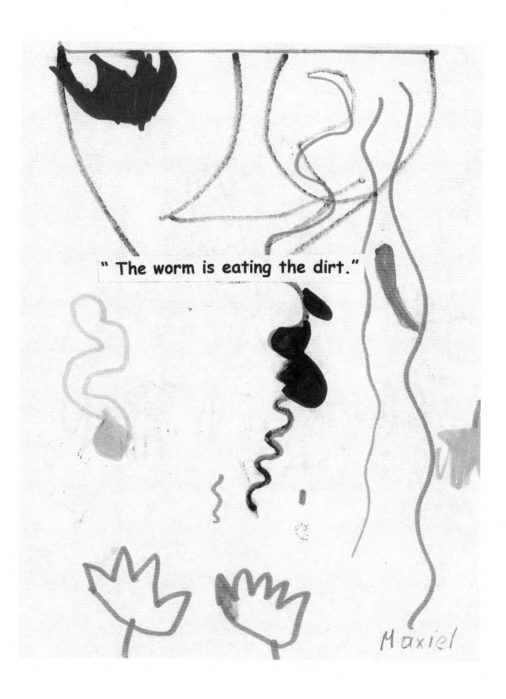

" The worm is eating the dirt."

Maxiel

USE REPRESENTATIONS TO DEEPEN LEARNING AND PROMOTE INQUIRY

- Build ability to communicate observations and ideas

- Focus on particular science ideas

- Build a culture of inquiry and collaboration

- Connect children's explorations from one day to the next

- Recap what has been learned at key points in an exploration

- Stimulate discussion in which children synthesize and analyze their work

FOCUS ON SCIENCE CONCEPTS BY PROMOTING INQUIRY

Responses that promote reflection

- Restate or rephrase
- Ask children for their ideas
- Accept ideas without judgment

Responses that promote analysis

- Ask for details
- Ask for examples, comparisons, or alternatives
- Ask "What if . . . ?"
  "Why do you think so?"
  "How do you know?"

RESPONSES THAT INHIBIT OR LIMIT THINKING

Responses that inhibit children's thinking

- Explaining the phenomenon
- Cutting children off
- Correcting children

Responses that limit children's thinking

- Leading them to the "correct" answer
- Telling them what to do
- Moving on too quickly

Settings for Science Conversations

- Talks with small groups

- Talks with the whole group

- Talks with materials or documents at the center

Documentation Panel

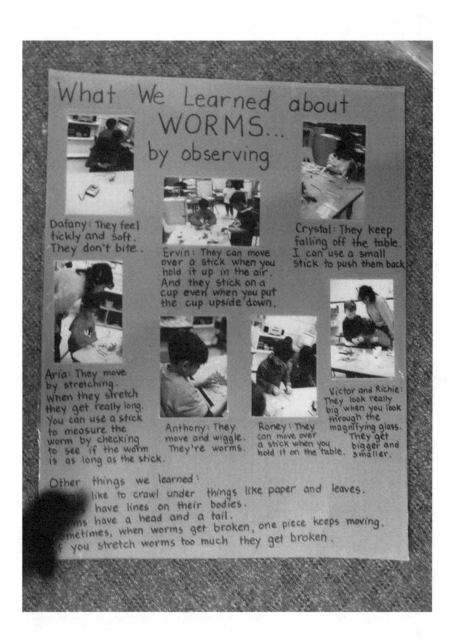

Documentation Panel Discussion Questions

- What is the intended message in this panel?
  What is the teacher trying to communicate?

- Where is the science engagement and learning in this panel?

- How well are these messages communicated?
  Where is the evidence of children's science learning?

- How would you change this panel?

DOCUMENTATION PANEL

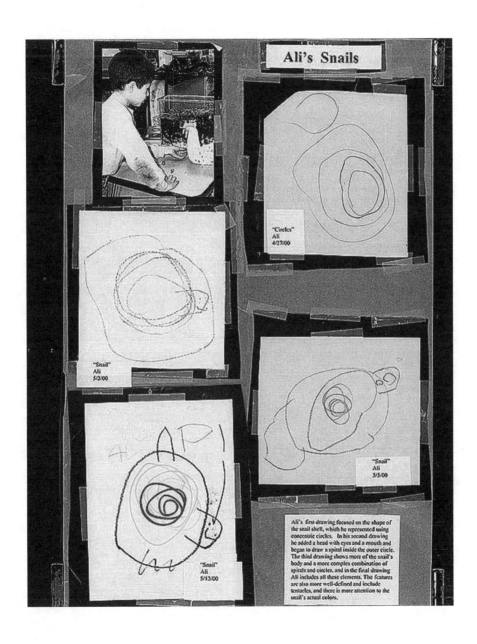

What Is a Science-Focused Documentation Panel?

- A poster that illustrates science inquiry and learning

- A multimedia presentation

- A story that can either take place over time or at one point in time

USES OF DOCUMENTATION PANELS

- Stimulate science talks

- Promote literacy as well as science

- Educate families

- Promote teacher and child reflection

Making Documentation Panels

- Identify a science exploration focus to illustrate

- Collect documents that will help tell stories

- Arrange documents on posterboard

- Add a title that focuses your readers

guided
discussions

Whether teachers are just beginning to use *Discovering Nature with Young Children* or are refining their practices as science teachers, you can use guided discussions to provide ongoing support and build collaboration among teachers. Through collaborative analysis of various materials, teachers build a deeper understanding of the science teaching and learning in their classrooms. By provoking inquiry and reflection, guided discussions support teachers as they engage in the ongoing process of refining their approach to teaching science. Guided discussions have the following advantages:

- **IMPROVE SCIENCE TEACHING AND LEARNING**
  These analytical discussions help teachers understand their role as science teachers and develop appropriate expectations for their children. Over time they develop a better understanding of the connections between their teaching and children's science learning. Improved practice is reinforced by child engagement and learning.

- **CREATE A COMMUNITY OF ADULT LEARNERS**
  Working in isolation, teachers often feel overwhelmed and very alone. By providing time and creating a structure for collaboration, teachers can share their resources and energy, while gaining a greater sense of community. This kind of support system encourages teachers to try out new ideas, share their experiences, and learn from others.

Once they have participated in the basic workshops, the guided discussions will keep enthusiasm alive, while supporting the implementation of *Discovering Nature with Young Children* in each teacher's classroom. Guided discussions have some common elements, which include the following:

- A group of teachers who are motivated to explore the approach found in *Discovering Nature with Young Children* and to talk about how it relates to their practice and to children's learning

- A leader who has identified learning objectives and is willing to commit to the group and its development

- Documentation from teachers' classrooms (including video clips or observations of teaching practice, children's work samples, or audiotaped conversations) to serve as common discussion points in group meetings
- A set of questions designed to guide the discussion, build connections between this approach and the documentation being used, help teachers reflect on their practice, and develop ways to apply new ideas to their work

Your guided discussions will be most successful under the following conditions:

- Discussions involve a small group of teachers (four to seven is optimal)
- Attendance is seen as part of teachers' regular responsibilities
- Time—an hour or hour and a half—is set aside regularly (at least monthly) for the discussions
- Discussions have a focus on practical aspects of science teaching and are structured so one builds on another
- A supervisor, mentor teacher, or other program leader is committed to planning and facilitating all of the discussions
- Leadership within the group is cultivated and the group becomes more self-sustaining

Selecting the right time to introduce guided discussions is also key to their effectiveness. They can be introduced at several points:

- **AFTER THE BASIC WORKSHOPS.** If you are working with a small group of teachers and want to move to a more informal setting after the basic workshops, consider starting guided discussions. Teachers will probably benefit from continual examination of the teacher's guide if they can focus on the stage of the teaching framework where they are currently working, either open exploration or focused exploration. Rereading sections of the teacher's guide, reviewing vignettes and work samples from the basic workshops, and sharing observations from their classroom will help them as they translate the print curriculum into their daily classroom life.

- **AFTER EACH ADVANCED WORKSHOP.** Guided discussions might also be offered in between the workshops with a specific focus on the teacher's application of the content from the workshop. In this approach, ongoing guided discussions are interrupted by workshops that provide new content. For example, if participants explored deepening children's science understanding in their last workshop, they might view a videotape from one of their classrooms, analyzing the children's engagement and considering possible next steps. Or they might read and discuss one of the articles recommended in the "Next Steps" box. One or two teachers can be responsible for sharing their classroom experience in each guided discussion. Stay on a topic for as many sessions as it takes for each teacher to discuss her work. Over time, teachers will begin to take some responsibility for planning the discussions. They will select topics, provide stimulus material, and plan discussion questions. They might select a focus that relates to their role as a facilitator of inquiry, such as encouraging representation or guiding science talks. Or they may want to better understand how to assess different kinds of child work by developing their observation skills or jointly examining work samples and transcripts.

Preparing for Guided Discussions

A successful guided discussion begins with thoughtful preparation. You will want to start by identifying teachers' needs and then determining appropriate goals, materials, and questions. For teachers who have participated only in the basic workshops, these discussions can provide a more in-depth look at the teacher's guide, a more thorough discussion of some of the video vignettes and work samples used in the basic workshops, and time to explore emerging issues on documenting children's work. Try not to let the focus shift to control issues in the classroom. These group discussions are about the teaching and learning of science. Remind teachers of this and suggest another forum for the other topics they bring up.

Teachers who have participated in the advanced workshops can examine their own documents, which will stimulate and guide their reflection as they adopt new approaches and will provide a vehicle for ongoing support and collaboration.

Use the "Sample Guided Discussion Plans" in "Resources" (p. 197) when you begin to prepare your meetings. These sample plans provide goals, recommended materials, and discussion questions for three different kinds of discussions. Copy and use the planning form to record your plans and reflections for each discussion.

Use the following suggestions to ensure the success of your discussions.

ASSESS TEACHERS' NEEDS

As you plan when and how to use guided discussions, you will need to take into consideration the teachers' backgrounds with curriculum and science teaching and the amount of previous experience they have had with *Discovering Nature with Young Children*. Some teachers may have a background in science or your program might be using a curriculum that embraces the same teaching approaches. These teachers might more quickly grasp the approach to science and science teaching, and they might be ready to share more sophisticated insights and their own experiences in a self-directed setting. Teachers without this background will need a more intensive introduction to the teacher's guide first. Use the "Science Teacher Development Stages" in the section on assessing teacher growth (p. 202) to determine appropriate goals for teachers.

An essential aspect of their work as science teachers will be elevating the science content in the children's explorations. They must understand these science concepts in order to recognize them in their children's work. After their hands-on experiences with these concepts in the basic workshops, the guided discussions are a great place to reinforce what teachers understand. Always talk about the science that is present in the documents being discussed, the concepts they are exploring, and what they understand.

It is also important to consider teachers' own perceptions of their needs. As you conduct the workshops, listen carefully to their questions and concerns. Provide opportunities for them to suggest topics they want to focus on. If they have particular interests, their motivation to participate will be high.

DEVELOP A GOAL THAT RESPONDS TO TEACHERS' NEEDS

A goal is stated in broad terms and reflects one aspect of the approach found in *Discovering Nature with Young Children* (such as to better understand how children use representation to deepen their understanding of science ideas). Use the "Science Teacher Development Stages" on p. 202 as you think about appropriate goals for teachers. Also remember to take their interests into consideration. It will probably take several guided discussion meetings to fully explore one goal, as there will often be multiple perspectives to explore and you will want each teacher to have time to discuss her classroom.

DEVELOP LEARNING OBJECTIVES FOR EACH GOAL

Learning objectives provide more specificity than the goal. That is, objectives elucidate the goal by articulating the major points that you want teachers to take away from the discussion. Each goal might have several objectives. For example, if your goal is to better understand why representation is important to science learning, three objectives might be the following: (1) recognizing children's science ideas in their representations, (2) understanding the relationship between media being used (drawing, clay, three-dimensional collage) and the qualities of children's representations, and (3) exploring the role the teacher can play in encouraging representation and using it to deepen learning. It is the objective that will determine the content focus, the appropriate materials to use, and your guiding questions.

SELECT MATERIALS

Select material that will illustrate the learning objectives and fuel discussion. Whether you select a video clip of a teacher engaging children in an outdoor exploration, a section of the teacher's guide, children's work samples, or a reading recommended in the bibliography, the resource you select should achieve the following:

- Challenge teachers' previous notions about science teaching and learning (These types of resources are more likely to provoke discussion than information that confirms what teachers already know.)

- Clearly illustrate children's engagement and science understandings, as well as the learning objective you have developed

- If using a video, feature a situation that represents an aspect of the *Discovering Nature with Young Children* curriculum

- If using a reading or case study, select one that contains relevant content written at a level appropriate for the teachers in the group.

As you prepare, become thoroughly familiar with the material. Consider the main message that the document conveys, how these ideas compare with teachers' current thoughts or practices, and how different teachers might respond.

DEVELOP DISCUSSION QUESTIONS

Develop discussion questions that will stimulate analysis of key points and practices. Create a core group of questions and a set of subquestions to raise if central points are missed during the discussion. Identify questions that will guide the discussion carefully from being descriptive to being analytical by following these four steps:

1. **BEGIN WITH GENERAL OPEN-ENDED QUESTIONS** about the document (such as, "What did you think about the article we read?").

2. **ASK FOR OBJECTIVE DESCRIPTION OF THE MATERIAL** (such as, "What do you see in this work sample? How would you describe its key features?"). Or you might ask teachers to take observational notes when watching a videotape and then review what they saw.

3. **ASK TEACHERS TO DRAW INFERENCES,** analyzing what they have seen by making connections between the stimulus and the content ideas (such as, "What exactly did this teacher do to encourage the conversation? What was the connection between the teacher's actions and the children's engagement? Did you see missed opportunities? What might you have

done differently?"). Always include some discussion of the children's science knowledge to reinforce the teachers' attention to the science concepts.

4. **FINALLY, ASK THEM TO DRAW CONCLUSIONS,** making connections to their own teaching (such as, "What connections can you make to the work you are doing in your classroom? Which of the approaches used here might work with your children? Which ideas generated by the group are worth trying?").

HELP PARTICIPANTS PREPARE FOR THE DISCUSSION

The teachers in your guided discussions can also prepare. You can help them by doing the following:

- Provide teachers with information about the content you will focus on beforehand to promote more thoughtful reflection. (For example, you might want them to read a portion of the teacher's guide or a related article or book chapter.)

- Share discussion questions, if you have them prepared.

Leading Guided Discussions

LAY THE GROUNDWORK IN THE FIRST MEETING

At your first meeting, spend some time as a group establishing the ground rules. Agree on a time limit and times to meet—keep in mind that regularly scheduled discussions have maximum impact. Ensure that the group knows that they are to listen respectfully to what others are saying and not interrupt. And let teachers know that a successful discussion depends more on what they have to say than on what you say. Rather, your role is to stimulate the discussion, keep the focus on science, summarize the group's thinking, and create bridges to the next level of questions.

FOLLOW THIS THREE-PHASE PROCESS WHEN FACILITATING GROUP MEETINGS

Phase 1: Open the meeting by briefly describing the content that is the focus for this discussion. For example, you might be examining a particular section of the teacher's guide or an aspect of the teachers' role. If you asked your teachers to read a section of the guide or a related article before they came, provide time for them to share what they learned from the reading and list their ideas on a chart for later reference. Add to their list any important points that haven't come up yet. Explicit presentation of the relevant teaching and learning content is necessary for thoughtful analysis.

Phase 2: Introduce and review the stimulus. Briefly introduce the material and its purpose, connecting it back to the content you have just reviewed. For example, if you are working on developing the ability to engage children in conversations, and teachers will be analyzing a videotape of a science talk, introduce the viewing by asking teachers to focus on the strategies that you have just reviewed with them. Teachers will tune in differently and ask different questions depending on how you focus their attention. If your document is print materials, such as children's drawings or a series of photographs, try to have several sets so everyone can easily review them.

Phase 3: Guide the discussion using the questions that you developed to help the group fully explore important points. Remember the four steps that guide question development:

(1) begin with general open-ended questions, (2) ask for objective descriptions, (3) draw inferences, and (4) draw conclusions. Leave a few minutes to summarize key points by distilling the thoughts and responses of teachers into several key points.

Keep the Discussion Focused on the Topic

Use these tips to promote full participation:

- Listen carefully and monitor teachers' body language to stay aware of how the group is doing. If you are not sure, check in with a simple "How are you doing with the discussion?"

- Ensure that each teacher has a chance to speak. Engage reluctant participants by making eye contact with them and smiling. Let them know through your body language that they have your support when they are ready to speak.

- Discourage anyone from dominating the conversation by moving the question to another person or by saying, "Let's hear from someone else on that issue."

- Encourage teachers to speak to each other, "Marie, you look like you have a suggestion for Joan. Let her know what you are thinking." Some teachers may be tempted to direct their comments to you or to wait for your response.

- Provide time after you ask a question. Teachers need time to reflect and come up with a thoughtful response. Your silence will communicate that it is their turn to talk and that it is alright for them to take time to think.

- Challenge ideas without challenging a teacher personally.

Build Communication and Leadership among Teachers

Follow Up with Each Teacher

Whether it is individually or in the next discussion, provide time for teachers to talk about how implementing these new ideas went in their classrooms. If you are addressing the same topic over several discussions, you will want to open discussions with some reporting on their successes and issues to set the stage for further dialogue. List issues on a chart and return them at the end to see what new implications might help address issues. If you regularly observe and have conferences with these teachers, these are ideal times to acknowledge the progress they have made and the impact they have on children's learning. At the same time, you can pinpoint ongoing issues that you might want to build into guided discussion goals in the future.

Encourage Teacher Leadership

As your teachers learn the culture and process for engaging in guided discussions, begin to give them responsibility for planning and facilitating.

- Support teachers as they learn to create documents of the teaching and learning in their classrooms. Provide equipment and help with videotaping and photographing. Interested community groups might help by making contributions for equipment or volunteering time to help in the classroom. Be sure teachers have varied materials for children's representation. Give them time to reflect and plan.

- Let teachers plan guided discussion meetings with you. Help them learn the questioning sequence as they use the guided discussion planning form.

- Take a supporting role as you give them responsibility for facilitating meetings. While you let them take the lead, be prepared to jump in if they want support. You might ask a question that redirects a conversation that is getting off track or move the focus from a teacher who is dominating the dialogue.

- Debrief with them after, allowing them to share their feelings and questions. Use the planning form reflection questions to guide the conversation.

promoting teacher growth through mentoring

The basic and advanced workshops and the guided discussions provide an effective social setting for learning about science teaching. Teachers will also benefit from individual attention that focuses on their own issues as they implement *Discovering Nature with Young Children* in their classrooms. A supervisor or mentor can play a critical role in providing this individualized support, helping teachers evaluate their efforts and build their capacity as science teachers.

The primary goal of mentoring is to guide teachers' development as science teachers through reflection on their practice. You will help them choose appropriate goals, document their work, analyze their practice, and modify their approach to science teaching and learning. Mentoring provides important opportunities to build teachers' ability to do the following:

- Understand the science concepts in the context of children's play, conversations, and representations.

- Evaluate the teaching strategies they are using and their impact on children's science engagement and learning.

- Examine documents from their classrooms (videotape, transcripts of conversations, children's work samples, photographs, and observational notes) for evidence of children's inquiry and science understandings, as well as evidence of teaching effectiveness.

- Make informed decisions about their next steps with children's inquiry.

Ideally, mentors understand early childhood development, the complex nature of inquiry-based science, and the science being taught, and are able to analyze classroom science events. Effective mentors serve as guides: they share what they see, their knowledge, and their expertise in an objective and positive manner, while challenging teachers' thoughts and pushing their practice to new levels of competence. A mentor might be a supervisor, a professional developer, or a teacher who has reached the stage of development where they are refining their knowledge.

Observation and conferences are probably the most important tools mentors have for providing individualized support to teachers. Documentation collected during classroom observations provides the basis for collaborative analysis of teaching and learning, as well as for planning the next steps. The mentor's understanding of the specific classroom context, gained through observation, is essential for guiding teacher reflection and self-assessment.

The outcomes of this work will contribute to the successful implementation of *Discovering Nature with Young Children.* To conduct effective observations and conferences, follow these four steps:

1. Establish development goals and objectives with each teacher.

2. Prepare for classroom observations.

3. Conduct classroom observations.

4. Discuss the observations.

Step 1: Establish Development Goals and Objectives with Each Teacher

Use the first visit to establish several development goals with each teacher. Select a goal to start with and develop a few specific objectives that will be the focus of the teacher's initial work and your observations. For example, teachers may want to work on their ability to facilitate science talks. Possible objectives might include asking open-ended questions while examining the snails in the terrarium or using strategies that encourage children's representational drawing. Use the following steps to develop goals that both you and the teacher agree on:

- Conduct an initial classroom observation using "Evaluating Science Teaching" from "Resources" in the teacher's guide. This will guide recording what you see when observing. Review the teacher development stages on pp. 202–203 to help you determine which parts of the form would be most appropriate to use with each teacher.

- Ask the teacher to use the evaluation form to reflect on her teaching and think about her goals.

- Meet with the teacher. Elicit her thoughts and share your observations. Together, determine the goal and specific objectives using the teacher development plan (p. 210). Use one form for each goal.

Step 2: Prepare for Classroom Observations

Successful classroom observations begin with planning. As you arrange for your visits, assure teachers that the goal of these observations is to support their growth as science teachers, not to judge their teaching for a high-stakes evaluation.

- Schedule a time to observe. Arrange a time when the classroom activity is in line with the teacher's current objectives. For example, if the teacher is working on facilitating large group science talks, schedule your visit to gain a full picture of a large group conversation.

- Conduct a pre-observation conversation with the teacher. Whether on-site or on the phone, get some background information to guide your observation. This information will be crucial when you begin to examine the teaching and learning.

Find out the following:

- The teacher's specific goals for children's engagement and learning

- Aspects of inquiry she expects the children to be engaged in

- Teaching strategies she will use to encourage and guide children's inquiry

- What has led up to these particular goals and activities

- The progress she feels she has made and frustrations she might feel in achieving her current goal

- Documentation (videotape, audiotape, or photographs) that might help illustrate this observation, as well as the notes you will take

Step 3: Conduct Classroom Observations

Use these strategies to develop an approach to observation that effectively supports teacher development:

- Check in with the teacher when you arrive. Without disturbing the classroom activity, find out if there have been any changes in the teacher's plans. Unusual circumstances will influence the flow of the day and what you can achieve in your observation.

- Document what you see and hear. It will be important to have specific information from your observation when you have a conference with the teacher. Take careful notes on paper that has been set up with three columns: child behaviors/comments, teacher responses, my thoughts. Separating your objective information into the child and teacher columns will help you make connections between the two later on. The subjective reactions you note in the right-hand column will help you remember the outstanding events when you plan the conference. Photographs (especially in series), video and audiotapes all provide clear evidence of children's engagement and are excellent supplements to your notes.

- Remain open and friendly. The classroom will function at its best when you are viewed as a friend. While maintaining your focus, engage in brief interactions with the children who are curious about your presence. "I am here because I want to watch you play," is a good response. It shows an interest in the children while letting them know that it is their activity that you are most interested in. Your interactions with children might model a particular strategy or test its effectiveness, or it might help you gain a new understanding of a particular child or dynamic. If there is a difficult situation and an extra pair of hands is needed, pitch in and help. The teacher needs to know that you are there to support her.

Step 4: Discuss the Observations

Timely, objective feedback will play a key role in a teacher's growth over time. Plan the conference soon after the observation. The events of the day will be fresh in your mind and the teacher's if you set the conference for the same day or the next. When you meet, invite the teacher to bring additional documentation of the events you observed. Children's work samples, a documentation panel, a class-made book, or a set of photographs can provide an additional lens into the teaching and learning in the classroom.

Many teachers have not had the benefit of individual support that is focused on their professional growth. They will need time to learn how the process works and that they can trust your confidence and intentions, especially if you are their supervisor. Start by letting them control the agenda for the conference. You might set the focus on *Discovering Nature with Young Children*. Then let them show you what is happening and talk about their accomplishments and the issues on their mind. Once they have overcome any defensiveness and have learned that you are a helpful resource, you can share your perceptions, ask more challenging questions, and involve them in goal setting.

Once you get underway, keep the science concepts and inquiry process in the foreground as you use the following process to guide the teacher's reflection:

- Reflect on the observation and plan the conference. Take time to prepare for the conference. Think about what you saw and heard in the classroom and about what it means for this teacher's development as a science teacher. In preparation complete the "Science Teacher Observation Synthesis" form (see "Resources"). Note the highlights of the interactions you observed in the child and teacher column. Select the events that are related to points you want to make or to specific events you want the teacher to think about. Consider the questions and comments that will encourage teacher reflection and problem solving. Note them in the box at the bottom of the form. Take time to think through how the teacher might react and what your response will be.

- Review the goals of the observation. Review with the teacher the focus you both agreed on and how you structured your observation. Keep the conversation focused throughout the conference. It can be easy to slip into a conversation about a sick child or the teacher's stressful life, but these topics will only divert attention from the teacher's development as a science teacher. You will have to be the judge when circumstances are important enough to modify the agenda.

- Open with an opportunity for the teacher to comment. Establish the value you place on the teacher's thinking by asking the following questions: "What did *you* think about the activities I observed?" "Were you pleased with how things went?" "Did you think your goals for the children's engagement and science learning were achieved?" Listen carefully to the responses. The teacher's perspective will give important clues as to how you proceed.

- Share your observations. Start by acknowledging places where you agree with the teacher, making specific connections between the teaching you observed and children's responses. Note the places where your perceptions might differ.

- Use available documentation to describe and analyze the events observed. Any documentation you have is data that can be analyzed. Use these documents to illustrate the descriptive points you and the teacher are making. Note the discrepancies in your perceptions and the teacher's, and what stands out in the data. As you begin to analyze the observed events, consider any discrepancies, the teacher's goals for the children, and the focus of her work with you. You want the teacher to do most of the talking, synthesizing her own impressions and your observations in order to assess her growth and needs. Use statements and questions to guide her reflection. Consider pursuing the following:

  - What the data says about the focus of her work with you—"You are working on strategies for facilitating science talks. What strategies did you effectively use in this activity?" "Let's look at the data and see what the children's responses were." Proceed to analyze the teacher's strategies in relation to the children's responses.

  - What the data says about student engagement and learning—"Let's look at this information and think about the science concepts being explored." Once identified, ask about evidence of the children's interests, questions, and understandings in relation to those particular concepts. Create a picture of the children's current understandings, their questions, and particular interests.

  - What the data highlights or the discrepancies in your perceptions—"I was amazed to see how much more Margarita is talking. What do you think has contributed to her new ability to participate in science talks and to the vocabulary she is using?" "We seem to have different ideas about what these children understand about the characteristics of the bean sprouts. I would like to better understand your thinking. Can you show me some evidence? Are there representations showing the parts of the sprouts or comments they have made?"

- Help the teacher plan next steps for her teaching and the children's learning. Once you have analyzed the observation, it is time to think about the implications for her teaching. You will want her to determine her next steps with the children and what she will do next in relation to the objectives she is working on.

  Start with the following questions: "What do you think your next steps should be with these children? How can you extend this experience and build their science understanding? What would you want to accomplish with these strategies? Why do you think these are the right next steps? How will they elevate the science and promote inquiry?"

- Close with goal setting and planning. It is now time to plan the teacher's next professional development steps. Should she continue to work on this goal? It is best to stay with one focus for a while, allowing the teacher to fully integrate new strategies and experience their effect. When it is time to move on to a new goal, select appropriate objectives. Finally, plan a few activities that will help her move forward. You might give her an article to read or suggest a classroom for her to observe. Her plans might simply be trying out things in her classroom. Once plans are made, record them on a teacher development plan (p. 210 in "Resources"), synthesize the major points of the conversation, and schedule your follow-up.

resources

Key Instructional Strategies

As you conduct the basic and advanced workshops, you will use four key instructional strategies:

- Encourage exploration of the immediate natural environment

- Facilitate reflection on the science in teachers' explorations

- Present content about science and science teaching

- Guide analysis of classroom documentation to create a bridge between theory and practice

When these strategies are interwoven throughout your training program, you will help teachers integrate the *Discovering Nature with Young Children* approach into their teaching practice. In these workshops exploration precedes the presentation of content so that teachers can connect the content to these recent experiences with nature and inquiry. When the analysis follows the science and science teaching content, it provides opportunities to make the content presented practical.

Below we describe each strategy, providing a purpose for its use and guidelines to follow as you use them in your training program. In addition, you will find strategies for effectively using the video vignettes.

ENCOURAGE EXPLORATION

These hands-on experiences provide adults with the opportunity to engage in inquiry and model, at an adult level, the children's investigations and experiences. They provide direct experiences with inquiry-based teaching through outdoor explorations, indoor investigations, representation, and data collection and analysis.

PURPOSE

- Review past experiences with the living world and draw connections to new understandings

- Experience the use of inquiry skills and science exploration in the same way the children will

- Begin to build understanding of the science concepts, the nature of inquiry, and the approach to teaching

GUIDANCE

- Your preparation is key to effective training. You will want to read the advance preparation instructions at the beginning of each workshop. The preparation will involve exploring your outdoor site and collecting the materials for the indoor exploration. You will also want to know what teachers will find so you can learn a little bit about these organisms. Read "Step 1: Preparing Yourself—Science" in the teacher's guide (p. 13) to help you understand the concepts that are the focus of these naturalist explorations.

- As you lead teacher-explorers, you will be modeling the approach to teaching described in the teacher's guide. Use that guide as a resource as you prepare and reflect on your teaching. In the instructions for the workshops you will find discussion questions and purpose statements that will help you maintain your participants' focus.

- The time frame we have created is our best estimate of how much time you will need. Feel free to adjust it based on your style and the needs and interests of your participants. However, it is important not to skip any of the activities as the exploration will have little meaning without the reflection, content, and analysis pieces or vice versa.

- Support everyone's engagement. As you observe what is happening during the hands-on explorations, be sure that everyone is engaged. Look for the participants who are hanging back or being dominated by another group member. Engage them by asking them what they have noticed or suggest a job they could perform for the group.

Facilitate Reflection

These large group conversations involve discussion of and reflection on the group's experiences during their explorations—group experiences provide the opportunity to learn from one another and draw conclusions from a much larger body of evidence. Teachers will have time to process their experiences in the same way they will do it with children, draw conclusions from the work of the whole group, and build an understanding of the power of reflection and collaborative thinking.

Purpose

- Connect the explorations to the underlying science concepts and inquiry skills

- Connect the explorations to the teachers' own teaching and their children's learning

- Articulate the teachers' current understandings

Guidance

- Listen carefully. You will be learning a lot about teachers' current understandings of the science content and their teaching of science. Note confusions that you will need to address now or follow up on later. Modify your future interactions to respond to teacher needs and interests, just as you would with children.

- Prompt teachers for fuller descriptions and explanations. You will help them expand their understanding as well as learn more about their thinking if you pursue a comment or question before moving on to the next one. Ask, "What else did you see? Why do you think this is so? Why do you think I did that?"

- Maintain the focus. Keep your ultimate goal in mind—to prepare teachers to use *Discovering Nature with Young Children* successfully in their classrooms. Each reflective conversation has an instructional purpose and a limited amount of time. Try to manage the time so teachers have an opportunity to discuss all of the important reflection questions.

Present Content

This strategy is your opportunity to formally share content. The content will be about science concepts and inquiry skills, specifics about *Discovering Nature with Young Children* and its approach, or descriptions of the teacher's roles. Presentations are supported by overheads and references to sections of the teacher's guide.

Purpose

- Begin to understand the *Discovering Nature with Young Children* approach to science teaching and learning

- Become familiar with the teacher's guide and the many resources it contains

Guidance

- Use the visual and print material that support these presentations. The references to the teacher's guide are important resources for your participants. By referring to them in your presentations, you help participants learn when and how to use them. The overheads will also help your visual learners stay engaged throughout the presentations.

- Make connections between the content of the presentations and the teachers' past teaching or naturalist experiences (for example, when you are talking about observing children's explorations, ask teachers which strategies they have successfully used in the past to document observations). When these connections are explicit it will be easier for participants to absorb the content.

GUIDE ANALYSIS

While the explorations and presentations are important, they will only have an impact on practice when teachers can make connections between what they are learning and their work as teachers. To help them make these connections, engage them in analyzing classroom documentation (such as the video vignettes, children's work samples, teachers' journal entries, and photographs).

PURPOSE

- Connect science content and science teaching to daily work with young children

- Build skill as reflective analytical thinkers

- Learn to see the science ideas and inquiry skills in the many forms of children's communication

- Build the ability to use documentation when assessing own science teaching as well as the children's science learning

GUIDANCE

- Familiarize yourself with the criteria in this guide that are being used to analyze each document or vignette. For example, you will want to review the content that is important for the analysis of each video vignette before looking at the tape. If you are going to be looking at children's inquiry, review the inquiry diagram and inquiry skills outcomes.

- Begin with description and move to analysis. Good analysis is built on clear ideas about what is being analyzed. Begin these conversations with a description of the documentation—observations of the behaviors and interactions on a video vignette or descriptions of the elements of a child's work sample or of the living things they saw outside. Ask guiding questions to help participants describe what they see, and then help them make connections to the criteria being used for analysis. For example, describing a child's drawing helps teachers to think about what the child has and hasn't noticed. Then, the teacher can think about what this means. Specifically, they can ask themselves, "Now that I have a better understanding of what this child knows, what does that mean for my next steps as a teacher?"

- Monitor small group conversations. When teachers are working in small groups, listen to the conversations around the room. You will get insight into each group's thinking and can troubleshoot with those that get off track. Interject a comment or a question to move a group forward, or sit down and facilitate their conversation for a while.

- Remember the science content and inquiry skills. Each classroom artifact or video vignette provides another opportunity for insight into the science content. As teachers see the science concepts reflected in various ways on video or in children's work samples, they will deepen their understanding of these science concepts and the inquiry process.

USING THE VIDEO VIGNETTES

Video vignettes have a special role in *Discovering Nature with Young Children* training. They provide a unique opportunity for teachers to see the science teaching and learning of other early childhood classrooms. While doing this, teachers begin to think analytically, connecting what they have learned about the *Discovering Nature with Young Children* approach to actual classroom work.

The teachers shown in these vignettes are at different stages of development as science teachers and vary in their teaching style. They all use important strategies and engage their children in a naturalist exploration, but they all miss opportunities as well. Use these vignettes to draw out important aspects of science teaching and learning, and to identify other approaches that would also be effective. The point is not to criticize or defend the teachers, but to use their work as a stimulus for talking about science teaching and learning.

Many of the children in some of these vignettes are English language learners. Their teacher is using strategies that are particularly effective in helping them communicate their experiences and ideas while learning English. You will find references to these strategies in the instructions so, when relevant, they can be highlighted with teachers.

Each vignette has been selected for a particular purpose, but also presents an opportunity to think about the science concepts in a classroom setting. Use questions that draw out the science present in the video in addition to the other things you want your participants to see—"What science was being explored here?" Reinforce the link between the teaching and the learning—"Why do you think the teacher did that? What did the children gain? How did it focus children's thinking on a science idea? How did it promote inquiry?" Also ask for specifics. Return to the video to show segments again to be sure everyone agrees—"Where did you see evidence of that? What was the child doing? What was the teacher doing?"

Use the vignettes more than once. There is a lot to see and think about and teachers will benefit from multiple viewings. Use them in guided discussions, or allow teachers to take them home or look at them with their colleagues. Provide guiding questions that give focus to the viewing. Use the vignette log that follows to plan ways of using each vignette so that it meets teachers' needs.

Video Vignette Log

> The workshop instructions provide additional information about each of these vignettes, including the following: key science concepts being explored, inquiry skills being used, and teacher strategies. The workshops also provide guidance for discussing the vignettes. If you are using a vignette with individual teachers or as part of a guided discussion, be sure to review relevant sections about the vignettes in the workshops and sessions in which they are used.

1. YOUNG NATURALIST INQUIRY (5 minutes)

This montage presents a view of the culture of inquiry in classrooms where the children are young naturalists—engaged in exploring plants and animals in their natural environments. Children observe living things over time and think about what their observations tell them. Teachers observe children, listen to their questions, and document what children say and do. Such snapshots illustrate children's in-depth, inquiry-based, exploration and the teacher's role as a guide. This montage, which serves as an excellent introduction to *Discovering Nature with Young Children*, is used in the first basic workshop, "Introduction to *Discovering Nature with Young Children*," and the first advanced workshop, "Creating a Culture of Inquiry About Nature." It might also be used for introducing families and community groups to *Discovering Nature with Young Children*.

2. OUTDOOR OPEN EXPLORATION (5 minutes 27 seconds)

This vignette, filmed in a Boston Head Start classroom, shows a group of five preschool children and their teacher engaged in an outdoor open exploration. The teacher, with clip board in hand, serves as the documenter—recording what children find and where they find it, as well as the children's ideas. She uses comments and questions to introduce the science concepts that children will explore more in-depth later: "Where did you find the spider? Maybe you can find animals that might eat the berries. What do you think the ants eat? How can we keep them alive?" Throughout the exploration, she teaches respect for living things and serves as a model, as she carefully observes and wonders about the living things that children discover.

This vignette is used in basic workshop 3, "Overview of Open Exploration." It might also be used for the following:

- Practicing how to observe children's engagement and understandings

- Discussing children's naïve theories and the ways teachers might respond

3. Focused Exploration of Bean Seedlings
(8 minutes 33 seconds)

This vignette filmed in a Boston Head Start classroom, shows five preschool children engaged in a focused exploration of their bean seedlings. After children remove the seedlings from the cups and paper towels, they carefully observe the seedlings, talk about what they notice, and draw pictures of them in their journals. The teacher provides guidance in setting up; she also supports children as they make careful observations and drawings of the bean seedlings. The children are all English language learners with original languages of Albanian, Farsi, Spanish, and Arabic.

This vignette is used in basic workshop 5, "Overview of Focused Exploration." It might also be used for the following:

- Discussing strategies for engaging second language learners in the science exploration and helping them communicate their observations and ideas (Guidance for this conversation is provided in the instructions for basic workshop 5.)

- Practicing observation of children that have varying abilities and understandings

- Having a more in-depth discussion of the teacher's role in promoting children's science inquiry and how it reflects strategies discussed in the teacher's role (in the teacher's guide)

- Considering next steps the teacher might take and how the investigation of plants might proceed

4. Exploring Worms (5 minutes 44 seconds)

In this vignette (from the same classroom as in vignette 3) five preschool children are engaged in a focused exploration of worms. Children are attentive as they observe the worms from their terrarium, noticing their physical characteristics and how they move. The teacher guides their experience, making sure they are respectful of the worms and stimulating their thinking about what they are noticing. These children are all English language learners. Their original languages include Farsi, Arabic, Serbo-Croatian, and Ibo.

This vignette is used in advanced workshop 8, "Deepening Children's Science Understandings" and in advanced workshop 10, "Assessing Children's Science Learning." It might also be used for the following:

- Discussing strategies for engaging second language learners in the science exploration and helping them communicate their observations and ideas (See guidance in the workshop.)

- Considering how the vignette exemplifies focused exploration or the strategies suggested in the teacher's role

5. Encouraging Representation (5 minutes)

In this vignette, five children are working at a table, making observational drawings of plants. The teacher interacts with three of the children, eliciting their ideas about their representations and encouraging comparison to the plants they drew.

This vignette is used in advanced workshop 11, "Encouraging Representation." It might also be used for the following:

- Practicing observation of children who have varying abilities and understandings

- Discussing strategies for encouraging representations and the ways teachers can use children's work as teaching tools

6. Talking about Worm Drawing
(1 minute 26 seconds)

In this vignette, the teacher uses Daphne's worm drawing to engage her in a conversation about worms. Daphne, a Spanish speaker, is particularly interested in their varying size and the teacher helps her with the language for describing those variations. Daphne also shares her ideas—believing that the biggest worm must be the daddy.

This vignette is used in advanced workshop 12, "Using Children's Representations as Teaching Tools." The vignette might also be used for the following:

- Discussing children's science understandings, language development, and representation abilities

- Discussing children's naïve theories and the effective ways teachers can respond

7. TALKING ABOUT PLANT REPRESENTATION
(2 minutes 10 seconds)

This vignette also shows a teacher in conversation with a child. The teacher encourages the child to talk about the differences between the two plants by describing features of the plants and the drawings.

This vignette is used, along with vignette 6, in advanced workshop 12, "Using Children's Representations as Teaching Tools." The vignette might also be used to discuss strategies for deepening children science understandings through conversations about children's representations.

8. SNAIL SCIENCE TALK (3 minutes 14 seconds)

In this vignette, a teacher engages her "snail observers" in a conversation over the lunch table.

The question they are pursuing is how snails move. Children take turns sharing their observations and ideas. The teacher carefully records what children say; she also probes for descriptive details, clarification, and additional information. All of the children are English language learners; however, several have learned quite a bit of English.

This vignette is used in advanced workshop 13, "Facilitating Science Talks." The vignette might also be used for the following:

- Discussing strategies for deepening children's science understandings through conversations

- Discussing strategies for helping second language learners communicate their observations and ideas

GUIDED DISCUSSION PLANS: SAMPLE 1

This beginning-level discussion, which focuses on understanding the *Discovering Nature with Young Children* teacher's guide, might be used with teachers who have only participated in the basic workshops. Others like it might follow and focus on other aspects of the teachers' guide.

OBJECTIVES

To better understand the open exploration section of the teacher's guide, discuss the following:

- What is the purpose of open exploration and what does the children's activity look like?
- What does the teacher do during open exploration?

CONTENT

Ask teachers to read the open exploration section of the guide. Begin the meeting by listing key points about open exploration with the teachers.

DOCUMENT MATERIALS

Video cued to vignette 2 or a video created in one of your classrooms.

SAMPLE DISCUSSION QUESTIONS

Describe: What did you see in this video? How would you describe the children's engagement? What about the teacher's actions?

Analyze: Why do you think the teacher responded in a particular way? How does it exemplify open exploration? What other connections can you see between the video and our list?

Prompt: Can you explain what you mean? Why do you think the teacher did that? How does it encourage inquiry? Or, what is the connection there?

Conclude: What does this mean for your teaching? What do you think you will do differently next week? Why? What do you want to accomplish with your students? How will you do that? How will you know when you have accomplished that? What evidence will you look for?

GUIDED DISCUSSION PLANS: SAMPLE 2

A discussion, like this one, that highlights a particular aspect of children's learning can happen at any time. It builds on a teacher's understanding after the basic or advanced workshops, providing new insight through analysis of a new stimulus or by reviewing a stimulus they are familiar with from a new perspective.

OBJECTIVES

To better understand inquiry and what it looks like when children are exploring living things.

- What is inquiry?
- What aspects of inquiry are three-, four-, or five-year-olds capable of engaging in?
- How does a teacher help children engage in inquiry?

CONTENT

Use the inquiry diagram and description from the teacher's guide. Review key points, writing them on a chart at the beginning of the meeting.

DOCUMENT MATERIALS

Excerpts from a teacher's journal (pp. 10–12 in the teacher's guide), video cued to vignettes 3 or 4, or a video vignette or series of photographs from one of your classrooms

SAMPLE DISCUSSION QUESTIONS

Describe: What exactly did you see the children doing in this video vignette?

Probe: Help them focus on a particular child by asking questions like, "And what was Victor doing?" Be sure they stick to describing the behavior, not analyzing the inquiry, and do not make inferences.

Analyze: So which inquiry skills were being used? Which science ideas were being explored?

Prompt: Can you explain why you think so? What did the teacher do to encourage Erin? Why do you think she did that? How do you think that influenced Erin's thinking? What evidence was there of that? What understandings about science were evident? Where?

Conclude: What does this mean for your teaching? What do you think you will do differently next week? Why? What do you want to accomplish with your children? How will you do that? How will you know that you have succeeded?

GUIDED DISCUSSION PLANS: SAMPLE 3

This discussion, which could span several meetings, helps teachers connect their teaching to children's learning. It should come after the teachers are well grounded in the *Discovering Nature with Young Children* approach and are refining their science teaching.

OBJECTIVES

To better understand how children use representation to reflect their science ideas.

- Recognize children's science ideas in representations where they have used various media.
- Select appropriate media, considering topic and children's diverse abilities.
- Use assessment of children's work to plan next steps.

CONTENT

Important ideas, video vignettes, and work samples from the two advanced workshops on representation.

DOCUMENT MATERIALS

Selected samples of children's work using different media from your classrooms or from workshops.

SAMPLE DISCUSSION QUESTIONS

Describe: Talk about samples one at a time. What do you see in this drawing? What characteristics of the worm has Mary illustrated?

Prompt: How has she used color? How many body parts has she represented? Repeat for several samples, varying child ability or media.

Analyze children's work: How do these samples differ?

Prompt: What is the evidence for how they differ?

Analyze teaching: Do these media help children communicate their ideas? What other media might be used with these children? How might you use this document in the classroom?

Prompt: Have you tried that media? Why do you think it will work here? What specifically would you do? What response would you hope for?

Conclude: What does this mean for your teaching? What do you think you will do differently next week? Why? What do you want to accomplish with your children? How will you do that?

GUIDED DISCUSSION PLANNING FORM

Name: _____

Date: _____

Goal: _____

Objective(s): _____

Pre-reading: _____

Content Focus: _____

Stimulus: _____

Questions that encourage description:

Questions that stimulate analysis:

Concluding Questions:

Your reflection on the discussion:

1. Describe the engagement of the teachers in this discussion. What insights did they share as they analyzed the stimulus material? What do they understand? What are their questions?

2. How would you evaluate the effectiveness of the discussion? Consider the appropriateness of the goal, objective(s), materials, and questions. What worked? What would you do differently next time?

3. What are appropriate next steps for these teachers? Do they need more time on this topic or are they ready for a new one? If you are moving to a new one, what will it be? Have the teachers given input into this decision? How might you involve them? Is there potential leadership emerging? How will you nurture it?

Assessing Teacher Growth

Taking time periodically to assess teachers' growth will help you respond to their professional development interests and needs. Assessment will be especially helpful when you are moving from the basic to advanced workshops and when you are planning mentoring or guided discussions. Use the following two tools:

- Science Teacher Development Stages—Describes knowledge and skills at three stages of development as inquiry-based science teachers. Professional development goals are suggested for each stage. Refer to these stages when you have assessment data and want to plan appropriate next steps.

- Evaluating Science Teaching—a tool for recording your observations of teacher practice. Use it to gather evidence on which to base decisions about next steps in professional development. Planning advanced workshops, guided discussions, and mentoring are all times when this information will be helpful. You might also want to use it to chart teachers' progress, adding evidence as teachers develop new skills. You will find some additional guidance on using this form at the end of the section on science teacher development stages.

SCIENCE TEACHER DEVELOPMENT STAGES

Teachers will go through a developmental process as they learn to use *Discovering Nature with Young Children*. This process can be defined in three stages: beginning, developing, and refining. Most teachers will likely start as beginners because they have very little experience facilitating an in-depth study of science with young children. Both the content and process of this type of science teaching will be new to them. While the approach to teaching science is new, it is assumed that they have a base in child development and developmentally appropriate practices that will inform their work as science teachers.

Understanding your teachers' current knowledge and skills will help you plan appropriate professional development and set realistic goals with individual teachers, as they will progress through these stages at different rates.

THE TEACHER BEGINNING TO USE *DISCOVERING NATURE WITH YOUNG CHILDREN*

- Current Knowledge and Skills—The beginning teacher is unfamiliar with many of the approaches used in *Discovering Nature with Young Children*. If she has experience in teaching science at all it may be setting up a science table, conducting isolated activities, or implementing themes that are rotated on a weekly or biweekly basis.

- Appropriate Goals for Teachers Beginning to Use *Discovering Nature with Young Children*—Teachers beginning to use *Discovering Nature with Young Children* will focus on following the step-by-step instructions in the curriculum guides. Possible goals include the following:

  – Beginning to understand the purpose, flow, and activities in the teacher's guide

  – Gaining a basic understanding of the science concepts being explored and the role of inquiry in science teaching and learning

  – Creating the environment as described in the teacher's guide, including materials, sufficient time, and space

  – Engaging children in the exploration and supporting their inquiry

  – Beginning to document children's science experiences

THE TEACHER *DEVELOPING* HER SCIENCE PRACTICE

- Current Knowledge and Skills—The developing teacher may still struggle with some of the same things the beginning teacher is experiencing, for example, how to get all of the children engaged. But she understands the goals, values the approach, and has some ability to engage children in inquiry-based science. Science engagement will be evident in the environment and interactions in this classroom. The children's interactions and the classroom displays will reveal a focus on plants, animals, or the outdoor environment. The developing teacher acknowledges children's science explorations and creates opportunities for children to reflect on experiences and ideas through discussion and representation.

- Appropriate Goals—The developing teacher is beginning to focus on improving her science teaching and promoting children's science learning. Possible goals include the following:

  – Continuing to build understanding of the purpose, flow, and activities in the teacher's guide

  – Building a deeper understanding of the science concepts and how young children build their theories and ideas

  – Creating a more "science rich" environment, including displays and accessible books that inform and stimulate investigation

  – Developing the ability to facilitate children's inquiry, balancing exploration with conversation and representation

  – Learning to use teacher's and children's documentation to stimulate inquiry and to connect children's day-to-day science activities

  – Learning to observe, document, and assess children's science engagement and learning.

THE TEACHER *REFINING* HER SCIENCE PRACTICE

- Current Knowledge and Skills—The refining teacher continues to develop her skills and abilities in all of the areas of the developing teacher and may still struggle with some of the same issues. For example, facilitating science talks that are focused on science experiences and ideas or understanding the science more deeply might continue to be challenging. But this teacher is comfortable with her use of the curriculum, the science concepts, and many of the teaching strategies. She uses documentation and reflection to guide her own development. She adapts her teaching, which is based on her understandings of the responses and needs of individual children as well as the whole group. Evidence of young naturalists' work permeates the classroom. The environment has many examples of children's work, naturalist tools for children to use, plants

and animals for study, and opportunities for small and large group science talks.

- Appropriate Goals—This teacher is focused on building the link between her teaching and the children's science learning. Possible goals include the following:

  – Using all parts of the teacher's guide to develop a system for observation, documentation, assessment, and planning

  – Building a deeper understanding of the science concepts being explored and how children's understanding is expressed in their behaviors and comments

  – Creating an environment that reflects children's current investigations

  – Developing the ability to deepen science thinking through interactions with children

  – Using documents more effectively to encourage children's reflection and further investigations

  – Integrating *Discovering Nature with Young Children* with math, language, literacy, and social goals

  – Describing children's science engagement and learning to families and others

  – Extending the exploration beyond the teacher's guide or developing explorations of new topics

EVALUATING SCIENCE TEACHING

On p. 205 you will find a tool to guide your evaluation of your teachers. Use it when conducting observations of each teacher to determine appropriate professional development and set goals for individual work. You might also want to use it to chart teachers' progress, adding evidence as teachers develop new skills. An observation is unlikely to provide all of the information you need to complete the evaluation. Arrange for a conference with the teacher and discuss what you have observed and some of the things you have not seen, for example, her observational notes or her work with her assistant or volunteers.

Different sections of the form are relevant for evaluating teachers at each stage of development.

As teachers become more skilled you will want to expand the aspects of their practice that you are focusing on. Use the following guidance when planning your observations:

- When evaluating beginning teachers, focus on sections I A, B, and C; II A 1 and 2; and II B 1.

- When evaluating developing teachers, continue to focus on the sections that you used for the beginning teacher and add sections: I D and the rest of II.

- When evaluating refining teachers, use the whole form.

EVALUATING SCIENCE TEACHING

Name: _____

Teacher(s): _____

Date: _____

Observer: _____

Teacher

Behaviors	Evidence
A. Teacher uses *Discovering Nature* teacher's guides to structure and sequence meaningful science explorations	
1. Follows steps in teacher's guide, using the teaching cycle of engage, explore, and reflect.	
B. Teacher uses environment to stimulate science exploration	
1. Provides materials and tools for explorations as described in *Discovering Nature* teacher's guides.	
2. Provides variety of two- and three-dimensional representational materials.	
3. Displays materials and books for easy access by children.	
4. Arranges furniture so children have enough room to work in open areas and on tables in groups of three to five.	
5. Creates displays at children's eye level that provide valuable information, relate to current science interests, and show children's own work.	
6. Provides choice times (thirty to forty-five minutes) with opportunities for children to engage with the science materials.	

Behaviors	Evidence
C. Teacher gives attention and positive encouragement to help children focus on science explorations	
1. Uses comments and questions to acknowledge activity and elicit ideas. Listens with genuine interest.	
2. Engages with children, modeling curiosity, play behavior, and use of tools. Invites reluctant explorers to play and helps them manage frustration by engaging them in problem solving.	
D. Teacher uses strategies that deepen children's science understanding and engage them in inquiry	
1. Encourages children's inquiry—observation, questioning, data collection, recording, and analysis. Offers new challenges as children are ready.	
2. Provides materials in varied media for children to represent an aspect of their experience or a developing theory and encourages the children to represent.	
3. Finds ways to focus children on science in their play.	
4. Facilitates science talks in which children share their experiences, ideas, theories, and conclusions.	
E. Teacher systematically observes and documents for assessment and teaching purposes	
1. Documents observations and interactions using various media, such as observation records, photos, audiotape and videotape, and collected work samples.	
2. Uses documents as teaching tools to connect day-to-day activities, stimulate and bring thinking forward, and launch new challenges.	

Children

Behaviors	Evidence
A. Children are engaged	
1. Use materials or observe living things to gain basic understandings of characteristics and behavior.	
2. Talk to each other and the adults about their science explorations.	
3. Engage in inquiry: observing, questioning, collecting data, recording, reflecting, and constructing explanations.	
4. Represent a part of their explorations—drawing, using collage materials or clay, or using their bodies to represent their work and scientific knowledge.	
5. Use resources (peers, books, Web sites, and so on) to extend their explorations and gain new information.	
B. Children are motivated and persistent	
1. Are eager to use the areas of the classroom that are designed for science explorations.	
2. Bring in items or tell stories from home that relate to their explorations.	
3. Show enthusiasm and interest extending to lunch table conversation, request reading from books and for dramatic play, and so on.	

Going Deeper

Behaviors	Evidence

A. Teacher helps other adults learn how to support children's science explorations

1. Supports assistant(s) in developing their ability to encourage children's science explorations.

2. Finds specific roles for classroom volunteers that support children's science explorations.

3. When opportunities arise, serves as a mentor to beginning science teachers.

B. Teacher extends own understanding of science and expands classroom applications

1. Extends this exploration beyond the steps in the teacher's guide.

2. Develops explorations of new topics.

3. Teacher seeks out deeper understanding of science content.

SCIENCE TEACHER OBSERVATION SYNTHESIS

Teacher: _____

Date: _____

Current goal/objective of teacher: _____

Teacher's goals for science and inquiry in observed activity

Children's Behavior/Comments	Teacher's Response

Questions or points to consider with teacher

SCIENCE TEACHER DEVELOPMENT PLAN

Teacher: _____

Date: _____

Strengths as a science teacher:

One goal for growth as a science teacher:

Objectives:

Activity	Time Frame	Resources Needed

Follow-up: (what and when)

References

SCIENCE AND TEACHING RESOURCES FOR INSTRUCTORS

See resource list for teachers below for additional titles. Note that the teacher resources are also valuable for instructors, and instructors should read all readings before giving them to teachers. You might also want to share some of these instructor resources with your teachers.

Bowman, Barbara, ed. 2000. *Eager to learn: Educating our preschoolers.* Washington, D.C.: National Academy Press.

DeVries, R., et al. 2002. *Developing constructivist early childhood curriculum.* New York: Teachers College Press.

Gallas, Karen. 1995. *Talking their way into science.* New York: Teachers College Press.

Goldhaber, Jeanne, and Dee Smith. 1997. You look at things differently: The role of documentation in the professional development of a campus child care center staff. *Early Childhood Education Journal* 25 (1): 3–10.

Harlen, W. 2001. *Primary science: Taking the plunge.* Portsmouth, N.H.: Heineman.

Landry, Christopher E, and George E. Forman. 1999. Research on early science education. In *The early childhood curriculum: Current findings in theory and practice.* New York: Teachers College Press.

Lind, Karen. 1996. *Exploring science in early childhood: A developmental approach,* 2d ed. Albany, N.Y.: Delmar Publishers.

Lindfors, Judith W. 1999. *Children's inquiry: Using language to make sense of the world.* New York: Teachers College Press

Moriarty, Robin F. 2002. Helping teachers develop as facilitators of three- to five-year-olds' science inquiry. Entries from a staff developer's journal. *Young Children* 57 (5): 20–24.

Osborne, Roger, and Peter Freyberg. 1985. *Learning in science: The implications of children's science.* Portsmouth, N.H.: Heinemann.

Perry, Gail, and Mary Rivkin. 1992. Teachers and science. *Young Children* 47 (4): 9–16.

Project 2061—Science for All Americans. 1999. *Dialogue on early childhood science, mathematics and technology education.* Washington, D.C.: American Association for the Advancement of Science.

Schweinhart, Larry J., and David P. Weikart. 1998. Why curriculum matters in early childhood education. *Educational Leadership* 55 (6): 57–60.

Wasserman, Selma, and J. W. George Ivany. 1996. *Who's afraid of spiders? The new teaching elementary science.* 2d ed. New York: Teachers College Press.

SCIENCE AND TEACHING RESOURCES FOR TEACHERS

Bourne, Barbara, ed. 2000. *Taking inquiry outdoors: Reading, writing, and science beyond the classroom walls.* York, Maine: Stenhouse Publishers.

Cadwell, Louise B., and Brenda V. Fyfe. 1997. Conversations with children. In *First steps toward teaching the Reggio way,* edited by J. Hendrick. Upper Saddle River, N.J.: Merrill/Prentice Hall.

Chaille, Christine, and Lory Britain. 2003. *The young child as scientist: A constructivist approach to early childhood science education.* New York: Allyn & Bacon.

Cohen, Richard, and Betty P. Tunick. 1993. *Snail trails and tadpole tails: Nature education for young children.* St. Paul: Redleaf Press.

Copley, Juanita V. 2000. *The young child and mathematics.* Washington, D.C.: National Association for the Education of Young Children (NAEYC).

Doris, Ellen. 1991. *Doing what scientists do: Children learn to investigate their world.* Portsmouth, N.H.: Heinemann.

Feynman, Richard P. 1988. The making of a scientist. In *What do you care what other people think?* New York: W.W. Norton.

Forman, George. 1996. A child constructs an understanding of a water wheel in five media. *Childhood Education* 72 (5): 269–273.

———. 1996. Helping children ask good questions. In *The wonder of it,* edited by B. Neugebauer. Redmond, Wash.: Exchange Press.

———. 1996. Negotiating with art media to deepen learning. *Child Care Information Exchange* 108: 56–58.

Harlan, Jean. 1992. *Science experiences for the early childhood years.* 5th edition. New York: Macmillan Publishing Company.

Hoisington, Cynthia. 2002. Using photographs to support children's science inquiry. *Young Children* 57 (5): 26–30.

Kostelnik, Marjorie. 1992. Myths associated with developmentally appropriate programs. *Young Children* 47 (4): 17–23.

Kupetz, Barbara N., and Meghan M. Twiest. 2000. Nature, literature, and young children: A natural combination. *Young Children* 55 (1): 59–63.

McIntyre, Margaret. 1984. *Early childhood and science.* Washington, D.C.: National Science Teachers Association.

Mitchell, Andrew. 1982. *The young naturalist.* London: Usborne Publishing Ltd.

NAEYC. 1998. Learning to read and write: Developmentally appropriate practices for young children. *Young Children* 53 (4): 30–46.

Osborne, Roger, and Peter Freyberg. 1985. *Learning in science: The implications of children's science.* Portsmouth, N.H.: Heinemann.

Owens, C. 1999. Conversational science 101A: Talking it up! *Young Children* 54 (5): 4–9.

Rivkin, M. 1995. *The great outdoors: Restoring children's right to play outside.* Washington, D.C.: NAEYC.

Shepardson, D. P., and S. J. Britsch. 2000. Analyzing children's science journals. *Science and Children* 38 (3): 29–33.

Smith, N. R. 1998. *Observation drawing with children: A framework for teachers.* New York: Teachers College Press.

Tudge, J., and D. Caruso. 1988. Cooperative problem solving in the classroom: Enhancing young children's cognitive development. *Young Children* 44 (1): 46–52.

index

The Young Scientist series was developed by a team of early childhood and science educators from the Tool Kit for Early Childhood Science Education project at Education Development Center, Inc. (EDC) and was funded by a grant from the National Science Foundation. The project was led by Ingrid Chalufour from the Center for Children and Families and Karen Worth from the Center for Science Education. Listed below are the key members of the team, all of whom contributed substantially to the work from its conceptualization to the final product.

INGRID CHALUFOUR, a project director at EDC's Center for Children and Families, has designed and conducted professional development programs for staff in child care programs, Head Start, public schools, and social service agencies for more than thirty-five years and is a principal developer of the Excellence in Teaching programs.

SHARON GROLLMAN, a senior research associate at EDC's Center for Children and Families, has developed educational materials for more than twenty years. Prior to coming to EDC, she was part of a research team in early childhood.

ROBIN MORIARTY is a research associate at EDC's Center for Science Education. Her work includes curriculum development, leading professional development programs, and working with early childhood centers. She taught young children in the Boston area for fourteen years before she joined EDC.

JEFFREY WINOKUR is a senior research associate at EDC's Center for Science Education. His work includes curriculum development and leading professional development programs for early childhood and elementary science education. He has worked in early childhood and science education for over twenty years and is an instructor in education at Wheelock College.

KAREN WORTH is a senior scientist at EDC's Center for Science Education. Her work includes the development of science curriculum and professional development programs, as well as consultation in science education for young children. She is also a graduate-level instructor at Wheelock College in the early childhood education department and has worked in the field of science and early childhood education for the past thirty-five years.

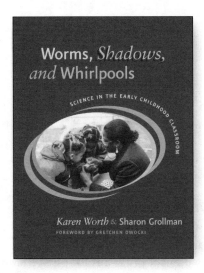